Seduced by Simplicity:
The Rise of Strongmen in Western Culture

A short introduction by K.R. Stonebridge

Seduced by Simplicity:
The Rise of Strongmen in Western Culture

ISBN: 9798866196722

Printed in the United States of America

Contents

Chapter 1:
The Backdrop of Complexity

Chapter 2:
The Allure of Simplicity

Chapter 3:
The Historical Precedence

How Past Strongmen Used Media and Public Sentiment to Their Advantage

Chapter 4:
Modern Media and the Strongman

The Role of Social Media, Echo Chambers, and Misinformation

How Strongmen Exploit These Tools to Present Themselves as the Sole Solution

The "Us vs. Them" Narrative and the Polarization of Modern Media

Chapter 5:
Economic Disparity and the Promise of Redemption

The Widening Gap Between the Rich and the Poor in the West

Strongmen's Promises of Economic Revival and Stability

Chapter 6:
Identity and Cultural Fears

Chapter 7:
Institutions Under Siege

Chapter 8:
The Role of Charisma

Chapter 9:
Opposition and Resistance

Chapter 10:
The Path Forward

Conclusion

Appendix A:
Profiles of modern-day strongmen in the West

Appendix B:
Further reading and resources

Introduction

Definition and Characteristics of a "Strongman"

The term "strongman" evokes images of muscular circus performers bending iron bars or lifting heavy weights. However, in a political context, it portrays a very different kind of power. A political strongman is typically characterized by his autocratic tendencies, his cultivation of a cult of personality, and his preference for rule by decree rather than through established democratic institutions. While the strongman archetype is not exclusive to any one culture or region, its manifestation in Western democracies poses unique challenges and questions. In this introduction, we will delve into the definition and characteristics that set these leaders apart.

1. Autocratic Tendencies

A hallmark of a strongman is a noticeable drift towards autocracy. Even if they rise to power through democratic means, such as elections, they often start eroding the very democratic structures that brought them into leadership. They might consolidate power by reducing the influence of other branches of government, suppressing opposition, or manipulating electoral systems. Their leadership style often involves making unilateral decisions without the usual checks and balances in place.

2. Cult of Personality

Strongmen are often charismatic individuals who create a larger-than-life image of themselves. This 'cult of personality' involves aggressive self-promotion, where the strongman is portrayed as the singular savior of the nation. This portrayal often relies on propaganda, state-controlled media, and sometimes even revisionist history. It's not uncommon to see their faces plastered across cities in murals, statues, or other monumental art. The narrative is straightforward: the country's success is deeply interwoven with the leader's personal success.

3. Rule by Decree

Rather than navigating the often complex waters of legislative processes, strongmen prefer to rule by decree. This allows for swift action, which can be portrayed as decisiveness. However, it by-passes the typical democratic methods of decision-making which involve debate, deliberation, and consensus-building. Over time, this can erode democratic norms and institutions, positioning the strongman as the primary source of authority.

4. Nationalism and Populism

Strongmen often harness the power of nationalism, appealing to a nostalgic vision of the country's "golden age." They promise to return the nation to its former glory and often blame internal and external "enemies" for the country's current woes. By presenting themselves as the voice of the "common man", they can tap into populist sentiments, pitting the general populace against per-ceived elites or minority groups.

5. Control Over Media

To maintain their image and control the narrative, strongmen often exert significant influence over media outlets. This can be done through direct state control, influencing advertisers, intimidation, or even the persecution of journalists. The end goal is to establish a media landscape that reinforces their worldview, suppresses criticism, and perpetuates their cult of personality.

6. Suppression of Opposition

Strongmen view opposition not merely as a political challenge but as a threat to their personal power and the nation's well-being (as they equate the two). As a result, opposition parties, activists, and critics face harassment, legal challenges, and sometimes even imprisonment or violence. Over time, this can result in a muted opposition, with critics silenced or coerced into compliance.

7. Militarization

A noticeable trait of strongmen is their fondness for the military and other uniformed services. They often bolster military spending, stage grand military parades, and position themselves as the nation's chief defender. This association with the military serves a dual purpose: it reinforces their image as protectors, and it ensures loyalty from a powerful institution that can suppress internal dissent.

8. Economic Control

While economic policies among strongmen can vary, they often involve significant state control or influence over key industries. Some strongmen nationalize industries or manipulate economic policies to favor loyalists. In doing so, they ensure that powerful economic actors are either under their control or are deterred from opposing them.

Conclusion

Strongmen are not merely authoritative leaders. They are a specific breed of leaders who centralize power, often at the expense of democratic norms and institutions. Their rise is frequently marked by populist rhetoric, a cult of personality, and an ability to tap into the sentiments of a significant portion of the population. While they might bring short-term stability or decisiveness, the long-term implications of their leadership often include eroded democratic institutions, suppressed opposition, and a society where power is concentrated in the hands of a few.

In the ensuing chapters, we will explore how the backdrop of complexity in the modern age provides fertile ground for the rise of strongmen in Western democracies. The juxtaposition of their simplistic solutions against a backdrop of intricate challenges offers insights into their appeal and the challenges of countering their influence.

The Paradox of Strongmen Popularity in Western Democracies

Western democracies, with their emphasis on individual freedoms, pluralism, and checks and balances, seem an unlikely breeding ground for the rise of strongmen. These systems were designed to prevent the concentration of power and ensure the voice of the minority. Yet, in recent times, there's been a noticeable trend of strongmen gaining significant traction and even assuming leadership roles in such democracies. This presents an intriguing paradox: How do leaders, often with autocratic tendencies, become popular in systems built on democratic ideals?

1. Disillusionment with the Status Quo

One of the primary drivers behind the rise of strongmen in Western democracies is the widespread disillusionment with the existing political establishment. Whether due to economic hardships, perceived inefficiencies, or corruption scandals, traditional political parties and politicians often face credibility crises. In such scenarios, strongmen emerge as outsiders, promising to "drain the swamp" or overhaul the system. Their narrative, rooted in anti-establishment sentiments, resonates with those who feel the current system has failed them.

2. Desire for Decisiveness

Modern democracies, especially in the West, are intricate systems with multiple layers of checks and balances. While this ensures power isn't centralized, it can also lead to perceived inefficiencies. Legislation gets mired in debates, reforms take time, and consensus-building can be a slow process. Against this backdrop, strongmen project an image of decisiveness. They promise swift actions and simple solutions, creating an allure for those frustrated with bureaucratic red tape or legislative gridlock.

3. Complexity and the Need for Simplicity

Western democracies, being at the forefront of globalization, face complex challenges. Issues like immigration, climate change, international trade, and technological disruptions don't have straightforward solutions. However, strongmen often distill these complexities into simpler narratives, usually identifying clear villains and promising easy fixes. This reductionist approach can be attractive, especially for those feeling overwhelmed or left behind in the rapidly changing environment.

4. Nostalgia and National Identity

Strongmen frequently tap into a nation's nostalgic feelings for a perceived "golden age." They promise a return to times when the nation was "great," often painting a picture that may or may not be rooted in historical accuracy. This plays into concerns about national identity, especially in the face of increasing globalization and cultural shifts. By positioning themselves as the defenders of traditional values and national pride, strongmen can galvanize significant support.

5. Media Amplification

While it's easy to assume that strongmen manipulate media, it's also true that media landscapes – especially in their current fragmented state – can amplify the messages of strongmen. The sensationalism, the "us vs. them" narratives, and the echo chambers created by social media platforms can reinforce and magnify the strongman's message, giving them a larger-than-life presence in public discourse.

6. Economic Insecurities

Economic downturns, rising inequalities, or fears of job losses, especially with the advent of automation and offshoring, have created genuine concerns. Strongmen often exploit these insecurities, blaming external forces, whether they be other nations, immigrants, or global institutions. By promising economic revival and protectionist policies, they appeal to those most affected by these economic shifts.

7. A Fragmented Opposition

A divided or fragmented opposition often inadvertently aids the rise of strongmen. When traditional parties or politicians are engaged in infighting or lack a unified vision, it presents an opportunity for strongmen to consolidate their base and project themselves as the only viable alternative.

Conclusion

The rise of strongmen in Western democracies underscores the vulnerabilities within these systems. It's a reminder that democracy, with all its merits, requires constant nurturing. The popularity of strongmen is not merely a reflection of their charisma or strategies but also an indication of deeper societal and systemic issues.

Understanding this paradox is crucial, not just to make sense of the current political landscape but also to fortify democratic institutions against potential erosions. As the subsequent chapters will delve deeper into the backdrop against which strongmen rise, it's essential to keep in mind that their popularity is a complex interplay of societal anxieties, systemic inefficiencies, and the charisma of the strongmen themselves.

Chapter 1: The Backdrop of Complexity

The Rapidly Changing Socio-Political Landscape in the West

The West, a region often characterized by its democratic values, economic prosperity, and cultural influence, is undergoing profound changes in its socio-political landscape. These shifts, driven by a myriad of factors, have transformed the way societies function, engage, and even perceive themselves. To truly understand the emergence and appeal of strongmen within this context, it's essential to unravel the complexities of this evolving backdrop.

1. The Digital Revolution and Information Overload

Arguably the most significant transformation of our times, the digital revolution has fundamentally changed the way people access and process information. The rise of the internet and smartphones has democratized information, allowing instantaneous communication and making news and views accessible to all. However, this flood of information also presents challenges:

- **Echo Chambers and Polarization:** With algorithm-driven platforms like Facebook and Twitter, individuals often find themselves in echo chambers where they are primarily exposed to views mirroring their own, leading to increased polarization.
- **Misinformation:** The sheer volume of information and the speed at which it spreads make it difficult to discern fact from fiction, leading to widespread misinformation.

2. Economic Shifts and Inequalities

Globalization, while offering numerous benefits like increased trade and economic interdependence, has also brought about economic disruptions:

- **Loss of Traditional Jobs:** Many Western nations have seen a decline in manufacturing jobs, often attributed to offshoring or automation.

- **Income Inequality:** The benefits of globalization and technological advancements haven't been evenly distributed, leading to stark income disparities.

3. Migration and Demographic Changes

The last few decades have witnessed significant migration flows, with people moving for better opportunities or escaping conflicts:

- **Cultural Integration:** Large-scale migration often leads to challenges in cultural integration, with concerns about national identity coming to the fore.

- **Perceived Threat to Jobs:** Migrants are sometimes perceived as competitors for jobs, leading to tensions even if the economic data doesn't always support these notions.

4. Rise of Populist Movements

Reacting to these changes, there's been a noticeable rise in populist movements across Western democracies:

- **Anti-Establishment Sentiments:** These movements often position themselves against the "elite", tapping into the disillusionment many feel with traditional politicians or institutions.

- **Simplistic Narratives:** Populist movements, by definition, appeal to the majority and often offer oversimplified solutions to complex problems.

5. Erosion of Trust in Institutions

Recent years have seen a decline in public trust in various institutions, whether it be the media, the government, or international bodies:

- **Scandals and Corruption:** High-profile scandals, often amplified by social media, have played a role in diminishing trust.
- **Perceived Inefficiencies:** Institutions, especially bureaucratic ones, are often seen as slow-moving and inefficient, leading to frustrations.

6. Global Crises and National Responses

Global challenges, whether they be financial crises like in 2008, the refugee crisis, or more recently, the COVID-19 pandemic, have had profound socio-political implications:

- **Nationalism vs. Globalism:** These crises often lead to debates on nationalistic versus global responses, with questions about sovereignty and local needs against broader global strategies.
- **Stress on Welfare Systems:** Crises often put pressure on welfare systems, leading to debates about resource allocation and national priorities.

7. Climate Change and Environmental Concerns

The undeniable reality of climate change has led to discussions, debates, and divisions:

- **Economic vs. Environmental Priorities:** Policies addressing climate change, such as transitioning from fossil fuels, can have economic implications, leading to tensions.
- **Inter-generational Divides:** Climate change discussions also reveal divides, with younger generations often more vocal about the urgency to address these concerns.

Conclusion

The Western socio-political landscape is marked by rapid changes, each with its own set of challenges and implications. While these shifts offer opportunities for growth, innovation, and collaboration, they also bring about anxieties, tensions, and divisions. Within this milieu, the appeal of leaders who promise certainty, clarity, and a return to "better days" becomes evident. Strongmen, with their simplistic narratives, often find fertile ground in such scenarios, positioning themselves as the antidotes to these complexities. In the chapters to follow, we'll delve deeper into how these backdrops make the rise of strongmen not just possible, but in many cases, even probable.

Economic Shifts, Technological Advancements, and Social Fragmentation

In the evolving tableau of the West's socio-political landscape, three crucial threads intertwine: the undulating currents of economic shifts, the relentless march of technological advancements, and the resultant fractures in the social fabric. This triad forms a significant part of the complexity backdrop, shaping perceptions, influencing decisions, and often, amplifying anxieties. By understanding these threads, we can better appreciate the appeal of leaders who promise stability in a world that often seems in flux.

1. Economic Shifts: From Prosperity to Uncertainty

Post World War II, the West experienced an unparalleled era of economic prosperity. However, as the decades rolled on, the sands began to shift, bringing with them challenges and uncertainties:

- **Globalization and its Double-Edged Sword:** The movement of goods, services, and capital across borders led to increased prosperity but also resulted in job losses in specific sectors, notably manufacturing in the West, as production shifted to regions with lower labor costs.

- **Financial Crises:** Events like the 2008 financial crisis left deep scars, leading to bailouts, austerity measures, and widespread disillusionment with economic establishments.
- **Wealth Inequality:** The benefits of economic growth began to concentrate among the top echelons, leading to significant wealth disparities, and consequently, social discontent.

2. Technological Advancements: The Digital Revolution and Beyond

The latter part of the 20th century and the dawn of the 21st have been marked by revolutionary technological advancements:

- **The Information Age:** The internet era democratized information but also presented challenges, from digital echo chambers to the rapid spread of misinformation.
- **Automation and the Future of Work:** Advancements in robotics and artificial intelligence have brought with them the promise of efficiency but also concerns about job displacement. The narrative of machines replacing humans in various sectors has been a source of anxiety for many.
- **Digital Surveillance:** Technology, while enhancing connectivity, has also led to concerns about privacy, data security, and the omnipresence of surveillance – both by states and corporations.

3. Social Fragmentation: The Cracks in the Mosaic

As economic landscapes transformed and technology permeated every facet of life, the social fabric began showing signs of wear:

- **Urban vs. Rural Divide:** Economic opportunities often concentrated in urban centers, leading to a divide between urban areas – usually more progressive and diverse – and rural areas, which often felt left behind.
- **Generational Gaps:** Technology created a divide between generations, with older individuals sometimes feeling out of sync with a rapidly digitalizing world, while younger generations grappled with the pressures of the always-online era.

- **Cultural Clashes:** Migration, both within countries and from outside, led to changing demographics. This often brought about rich cultural exchanges but also tensions, as questions about national identity, integration, and cultural preservation came to the fore.

The Interplay and Its Implications

It's crucial to understand that these three threads don't operate in isolation. There's a complex interplay:

- **Economic Discontent and Technology:** While technological advancements drive economic growth, they can also exacerbate economic disparities. For instance, tech hubs in specific cities lead to localized prosperity but can leave other regions feeling economically stagnant.

- **Technology and Social Fragmentation:** The digital age, while connecting people globally, can sometimes lead to local disconnections. Physical communities get replaced by virtual ones, leading to a change in the nature of social interactions.

- **Economic Anxieties and Social Tensions:** Economic uncertainties often manifest in social discontent. When people are anxious about their economic future, it's easier to find scapegoats, whether they be immigrants, global institutions, or even technological advancements.

Conclusion

The tapestry of the West's backdrop of complexity is rich and intricate. Economic shifts, technological advancements, and social fragmentation are but threads in this tapestry, albeit significant ones. Together, they create a landscape marked by opportunities and challenges, hopes and anxieties, progress and resistance. In such a scenario, the allure of leaders who promise clarity, who offer black and white solutions in a grayscale world, becomes both understandable and formidable. As we continue our exploration, we'll see how these backgrounds provide fertile ground for strongmen, who, with their simplistic narratives, promise to navigate this complexity on behalf of those who feel lost in its maze.

The Average Citizen's Feeling of Powerlessness and Information Overload

In the age of digital democratization and unprecedented access to knowledge, it would be reasonable to assume that the average citizen in the West feels empowered, enlightened, and engaged. However, the reality presents a contrasting picture. Many individuals express feelings of powerlessness in the face of institutional enormity and report being overwhelmed by the deluge of information available. This paradoxical juxtaposition of enhanced access yet increased feelings of detachment and disillusionment forms a critical facet of our exploration into the backdrop of complexity.

1. The Illusion of Information Abundance

The internet promised an era where information would be at one's fingertips, breaking down barriers and ensuring a more informed populace:

- **Overwhelm and Saturation:** While data is abundant, the sheer volume often leads to an information overload. With countless articles, news sources, blogs, and social media posts vying for attention every day, discerning relevant from redundant becomes challenging.

- **Paradox of Choice:** Psychologist Barry Schwartz's idea that an abundance of choice leads to paralysis and dissatisfaction finds resonance here. Too much information can lead to decision fatigue and a reluctance to engage.

2. Misinformation and Distrust

In an age characterized by the term 'post-truth', discerning fact from fiction has never been more challenging:

- **Fake News and Echo Chambers:** The algorithms powering platforms like Facebook and Twitter often create echo chambers, where users are repeatedly exposed to similar views, reinforcing existing beliefs and seldom challenging them. This environment is ripe for the spread of misinformation.

- **Distrust in Traditional Media:** Accusations of bias, instances of high-profile retractions, and the race for sensationalism have eroded trust in traditional media institutions.

3. Power Dynamics and Institutional Cynicism

While the digital age has empowered individuals in many ways, the larger power dynamics still skew towards established institutions:

- **Perceived Opaqueness:** The intricacies of bureaucratic processes, legislative nuances, and policy formulations can often seem opaque to the average citizen, fostering feelings of exclusion.

- **Economic Disparities:** As wealth gets increasingly concentrated and big corporations hold significant sway, many individuals feel that their voice and concerns are secondary, leading to feelings of powerlessness.

4. The Demands of Modern Life

The pace of modern life, with its demands and pressures, leaves little time for civic engagement:

- **Time Poverty:** Between jobs, familial responsibilities, and personal commitments, finding time to stay informed, let alone actively participate in civic processes, becomes challenging.

- **Mental Bandwidth:** Continuous information consumption, the pressures of modern living, and the challenges of economic survival consume significant mental bandwidth, leaving little cognitive space for active civic engagement.

5. Political Polarization and Apathy

The increasing polarization in political landscapes has further implications:

- **Us vs. Them:** With discourse becoming more binary and less nuanced, many find themselves disillusioned, feeling that they don't fit neatly into the polarized categories.

- **Apathy:** Continuous confrontations, partisan politics, and the seeming inability of leaders to find common ground can lead to political apathy. The sentiment that "nothing ever changes" becomes prevalent.

6. Fragmented Communities and Diminishing Social Capital

Traditional community structures have witnessed fragmentation:

- **Digital Over Physical:** While online communities are thriving, physical, local communities are weakening. This diminishes social capital — the networks, norms, and trust that facilitate cooperation for mutual benefit.

- **Anonymity and Isolation:** Urban living, characterized by anonymity, and the shift towards digital interactions often result in feelings of isolation, further exacerbating the feeling of being just a small, inconsequential cog in a vast machine.

Conclusion

The feelings of powerlessness and information overload among average citizens in the West, despite unparalleled access to information and tools for empowerment, underscore the complexities of the modern era. It's a milieu marked by contrasts — empowerment vs. powerlessness, information vs. misinformation, engagement vs. apathy. In such a scenario, the appeal of leaders who claim to understand these complexities, who promise to represent the 'voiceless' and offer clarity amidst the chaos, becomes both potent and understandable. They tap into these very feelings, positioning themselves as the antidote to the average citizen's woes. As this exploration continues, it becomes evident that the backdrop of complexity is not just about broad socio-political shifts, but also about individual feelings, perceptions, and experiences.

Chapter 2:
The Allure of Simplicity

Psychological Underpinnings: The Comfort of Clarity and Decisiveness

As we delve deeper into the allure of simplicity that strongmen leaders project, it's essential to understand the psychological foundations that contribute to their appeal. At the heart of this attraction lies an inherent human yearning: the comfort derived from clarity and decisiveness. In an era marked by ambiguities, uncertainties, and a torrent of information, the psyche often gravitates towards that which appears resolute, unambiguous, and confident.

1. The Cognitive Ease of Black and White

Humans, by their evolutionary design, prefer cognitive ease over cognitive strain:

- **Mental Shortcuts:** Our brains are wired to take shortcuts, termed as heuristics, to process information efficiently. Leaders who present issues in clear, black-and-white terms reduce the cognitive load required to understand complex issues.

- **Avoidance of Ambiguity:** Ambiguities often produce discomfort. A leader who offers a clear, unambiguous stance, even if overly simplistic, provides a psychological refuge from the discomfort of uncertainty.

2. The Decisiveness Quotient

In times of crisis or perceived threats, decisiveness becomes an even more prized trait:

- **Action Over Inaction:** Decisive leaders, by their very nature, give the impression of action. This can be comforting for many, as action, even if potentially misguided, feels better than perceived stagnation or indecisiveness.

- **Predictability:** Decisive leaders often exude a sense of predictability in their actions. This can be reassuring in times of change, even if the actual outcomes of their decisions might be unpredictable.

3. The Desire for Strong Leadership During Turbulence

Historical and psychological analyses often reveal a pattern:

- **Seeking Saviors:** In turbulent times, be it due to economic downturns, perceived cultural shifts, or external threats, there's a marked inclination among populations to lean towards leaders who project strength and assurance.

- **Protection and Security:** Strongmen leaders often position themselves as protectors of the nation, its values, or a particular way of life. This taps into a primal human need for security and safety.

4. The Power of Certainty in an Uncertain World

Certainty, or even the illusion of it, has profound psychological implications:

- **Reduced Anxiety:** Uncertainty can lead to anxiety. Leaders who project certainty can inadvertently act as an anxiety buffer for many individuals, providing a semblance of stability.

- **Validation of Pre-existing Beliefs:** A leader who exudes confidence in their beliefs can validate those held by their followers, further solidifying their support base.

5. Affiliation and Belongingness

Humans have an intrinsic need to belong:

- **Us vs. Them Dichotomy:** Strongmen often create a distinct in-group and out-group. This provides their supporters with a clear sense of belonging, reinforcing affiliative bonds.
- **Collective Identity:** By presenting clear, often nationalistic or cultural narratives, such leaders offer a collective identity that many find appealing and unifying.

6. Simplicity as a Counter to Information Overload

In an age of digital deluge:

- **Ease of Digestion:** Simplified narratives are easier to digest, share, and rally behind, especially in the age of bite-sized information and soundbites.
- **Reduction of Cognitive Dissonance:** When confronted with conflicting information, the mind experiences discomfort. Leaders who offer simple, unwavering narratives reduce the chances of such dissonance.

Conclusion

The psychological allure of leaders who provide clarity and showcase decisiveness cannot be understated. It taps into fundamental human needs and desires — the need for cognitive ease, the yearning for predictability amidst chaos, the primal instinct for safety, and the profound wish to belong and affiliate.

While these underpinnings don't justify the often reductive and potentially harmful solutions that such leaders might propose, they provide insights into their widespread appeal. Understanding these psychological nuances is crucial, not just for academic or political analysis, but for societies to introspect, address underlying anxieties, and foster a more informed, discerning citizenry. As the adage goes, "Know thyself." In understanding the allure of simplicity, societies might find the keys to building more inclusive, nuanced, and resilient democratic structures.

The Appeal of Clear Enemies and Uncomplicated Solutions

In the theater of politics, one of the most compelling narratives often involves the identification of clear adversaries and the proposal of straightforward solutions. This approach can be seen in the rise of many strongmen leaders and the groundswell of their popularity. Why does this narrative hold such sway in the public psyche? Delving into the allure of simplicity, the dynamics of clear enemies and uncomplicated solutions emerge as potent psychological and sociological tools.

1. Clarity Amidst Chaos

The modern world, with its complex geopolitical dynamics, socio-economic intricacies, and cultural amalgamations, is inherently chaotic:

- **Simplification for Understanding:** Identifying clear enemies or scapegoats simplifies the narrative. It provides an easily digestible reason for the challenges a society faces, making the world seem less capricious.

- **Attribution of Blame:** When there's a distinct adversary, there's a clear direction to point fingers, channeling public frustration and anger towards an external entity.

2. The Psychological Comfort of an "Other"

Throughout history, the concept of the "other" has been a prevalent tool:

- **In-group Cohesion:** By defining an out-group or an enemy, in-group cohesion is enhanced. The distinctions between 'us' and 'them' create a stronger bond among the in-group members.

- **Diversion:** A clear enemy can divert attention from internal problems, deficiencies, or inadequacies. Instead of introspection, the focus remains external.

3. The Promise of Quick Fixes

In an era of instant gratification, the appeal of immediate solutions is immense:

- **Impatience with Bureaucracy:** Slow-moving bureaucratic processes, while often necessary for thorough decision-making, can be perceived as inefficiency. Strongmen proposing quick fixes can seem refreshing.
- **Hope and Optimism:** Uncomplicated solutions, even if unrealistic, can foster hope. The promise of rapid, transformative change can galvanize public support.

4. The Narrative Power of the Hero vs. Villain Archetype

This narrative, as old as storytelling itself, remains potent:

- **Relatability:** The hero vs. villain archetype is universally recognizable, tapping into deep-seated cultural and psychological patterns.
- **Moral Clarity:** This narrative offers clear moral stances, with the leader positioned as the hero and the identified enemies as villains. Such clarity can be reassuring.

5. Cognitive Ease and Cognitive Closure

Humans often seek mental comfort and clarity:

- **Reduction of Cognitive Load:** Simplified narratives and solutions reduce the cognitive effort required to understand and process information.
- **Achieving Cognitive Closure:** Clear enemies and solutions offer a sense of cognitive closure, reducing feelings of uncertainty and ambiguity.

6. Reinforcement through Media and Propaganda

The power of messaging cannot be underestimated:

- **Repetition and Affirmation:** Through controlled media or persuasive propaganda, the narrative of clear enemies and straightforward solutions can be repeated and affirmed, embedding it deeper into the public consciousness.
- **Creation of Echo Chambers:** In today's digital age, algorithm-driven platforms can create echo chambers, where individuals are repeatedly exposed to the same narrative, reinforcing their beliefs.

Conclusion

The allure of identifying clear enemies and offering uncomplicated solutions lies at the intersection of psychology, sociology, and political strategy. Such narratives provide cognitive ease, reinforce group identities, offer hope, and tap into deeply ingrained storytelling archetypes. However, the world's challenges are seldom black and white, and the complexities they present rarely have simple solutions.

It is crucial for democratic societies to recognize the seductive power of such narratives and foster a culture of critical thinking, introspection, and nuanced understanding. This would not only reduce the susceptibility to over-simplistic narratives but also strengthen the fabric of the society to tackle challenges in a more holistic and collaborative manner. The allure of simplicity might be compelling, but the embrace of complexity, with all its challenges, remains essential for progress.

Comparing Strongmen's Messaging to That of More Moderate Politicians

The political landscape is vast and varied, housing a spectrum of leaders who span from the authoritarian strongmen to the more moderate, consensus-driven politicians. While they all aim to inspire, lead, and garner support, their messaging strategies can vastly differ. Diving deeper into Chapter 2's theme, "The Allure of

Simplicity", a comparative exploration of the messaging between strongmen and moderate politicians is crucial in understanding the breadth of political communication.

1. Tone and Tenor

Strongmen: Their messaging often exudes confidence, decisiveness, and authority. The tone is assertive, often combative, positioning themselves as the sole saviors or champions against perceived threats or enemies.

Moderate Politicians: They typically adopt a more conciliatory and collaborative tone. Their messaging emphasizes dialogue, cooperation, and mutual understanding.

2. Complexity vs. Simplicity

Strongmen: Their narratives often simplify complex issues, presenting them in binary terms. The solutions they propose, though seemingly straightforward, may often be reductionist, overlooking the intricacies of the issue.

Moderate Politicians: They tend to acknowledge the complexity of challenges, emphasizing the need for multifaceted solutions. Their messaging often seeks to educate and bring nuances to the forefront.

3. Emotional Appeal vs. Rational Discourse

Strongmen: Rely heavily on emotional appeals. Their speeches and communications often evoke strong emotions, be it fear, pride, anger, or hope. They are masters at tapping into the populace's emotional pulse.

Moderate Politicians: While not devoid of emotional resonance, they lean more towards rational discourse. Data, evidence, and logical reasoning form the cornerstone of their messaging.

4. Inclusivity vs. Exclusivity

Strongmen: Their messaging often creates a distinct in-group and out-group, emphasizing the differences and stoking divisions. This 'us vs. them' dynamic is a frequent tool, be it against external entities, certain demographics, or ideological opponents.

Moderate Politicians: Prioritize inclusivity. They emphasize unity, shared values, and collective aspirations, aiming to bridge divides rather than accentuate them.

5. Responsiveness vs. Authoritativeness

Strongmen: Often project an image of unyielding authority. Feedback or criticism is not only unappreciated but often suppressed or retaliated against. Their word is portrayed as the ultimate truth.

Moderate Politicians: Adopt a more responsive approach. They are more open to feedback, criticism, and evolving their stance based on new information or public sentiment.

6. Messaging Channels

Strongmen: Often prefer direct channels of communication with their base. This could be through rallies, personal social media platforms, or state-controlled media. The objective is to have an unfiltered, direct line to their supporters.

Moderate Politicians: While also utilizing direct channels, they often engage more with independent media, participate in open debates, and encourage multifaceted discussions on platforms that they might not control.

7. Consistency vs. Flexibility

Strongmen: Prioritize message consistency, even in the face of new information. This aligns with their portrayal of unwavering confidence and authority.

Moderate Politicians: While valuing consistency, they show a greater willingness to adapt, evolve, or even retract their positions based on evidence, changing circumstances, or public opinion.

8. Personal Branding

Strongmen: Heavily emphasize personal branding. Their narrative often intertwines with the nation's destiny or the fate of the people. The line between the individual and the office they hold often blurs.

Moderate Politicians: While personal branding is essential, there's a clearer distinction between the individual and the office. The emphasis is more on institutional strength than personal prowess.

Conclusion

The dichotomy in messaging between strongmen and more moderate politicians illuminates the vast spectrum of political communication. While strongmen rely on emotional resonance, simplicity, and a combative stance, moderate politicians lean towards rational discourse, inclusivity, and collaboration.

Understanding these distinctions is vital for the electorate, allowing them to discern the motivations, implications, and potential outcomes of the messages they receive. As the political landscape continues to evolve, so will the strategies of communication. Yet, the essence of these strategies, rooted in the allure of simplicity or the embrace of complexity, will remain pivotal in shaping political narratives and the course of nations.

Chapter 3: The Historical Precedence

Historical Examples of Strongmen in the West and the Contexts of Their Rises

From the annals of history, the Western world showcases various leaders who, with their charismatic personas, exploited societal discontent, economic downturns, or political instability to consolidate power. Chapter 3, "The Historical Precedence," delves into a selection of these figures, illuminating the backdrop of their ascendance.

1. Benito Mussolini (Italy)

Context: After World War I, Italy grappled with economic difficulties, political fragmentation, and widespread unrest. The government's perceived ineptitude in the post-war milieu disheartened the Italians.

Rise: Mussolini's narrative of restoring stability and strength resonated powerfully. With his Blackshirt paramilitary squads, he curbed opposition, often violently. The 1922 March on Rome cemented his reign, culminating in his installment as Prime Minister. Mussolini envisioned a return to Italy's past glories, invoking nationalism and the rebirth of the Roman Empire.

2. Adolf Hitler (Germany)

Context: Germany's World War I defeat and the punitive Treaty of Versailles resulted in economic woes, escalating unemployment, and a wounded national pride.

Rise: As the Nazi Party's face, Hitler tapped into the German psyche, stoking despair and resentment. By casting blame on Jews, communists, and perceived internal foes, he propagated fervent nationalism. By 1933, through astute political strategy, Hitler was the Chancellor, eventually dismantling the Weimar Republic and heralding the Third Reich.

3. Francisco Franco (Spain)

Context: Early 20ᵗʰ-century Spain oscillated between political extremities, marked by swift regime changes and a widening left-right chasm.

Rise: Franco, an influential general during the Spanish Civil War (1936-1939), led the Nationalist forces against the incumbent Republican government. Aided by Fascist Italy and Nazi Germany, his victory saw the dawn of a dictatorship that persisted until 1975. Franco's rule emphasized traditionalism, suppressing regional identities and freedoms.

4. António de Oliveira Salazar (Portugal)

Context: Early 1900s Portugal, transitioning from monarchy to an unstable republic, battled economic and political turmoil.

Rise: Salazar's journey from the Finance Minister to the Prime Minister by 1932 was marked by his introduction of the authoritarian "Estado Novo" (New State). Prioritizing Catholic tenets and staunch anti-communism, Salazar's era saw Portugal's World War II neutrality and resistance to decolonization demands, leading to protracted colonial wars.

5. Joseph McCarthy (United States)

Context: The Cold War's initial phase in the 1950s, marked by a profound fear of communism and potential Soviet espionage, set the stage for political witch hunts in the US.

Rise: Senator McCarthy's assertion of possessing a list of government-affiliated communists spearheaded the infamous McCarthy hearings. Many faced unwarranted accusations, resulting in tarnished reputations and deep-seated paranoia. While McCarthy's clout diminished by the mid-1950s, "McCarthyism" endures as a symbol of baseless vilification.

6. Donald Trump (United States)

Context: The early 21st century saw the US grappling with economic disparities, fears of job losses due to globalization, political polarization, and issues related to immigration and national identity.

Rise: Trump, a businessman-turned-politician, successfully tapped into a segment of the American populace feeling marginalized and voiceless. With a promise to "Make America Great Again," he championed an America-first approach, questioning established international alliances, and adopting a combative stance against perceived adversaries, both domestic and international. His unfiltered style, often bypassing traditional media through platforms like Twitter, solidified his base and led to his presidential win in 2016.

Conclusion

The chronicles of these leaders, while rooted in their unique socio-political contexts, echo certain universals:

1. Their emergence during times of national unrest or transition.

2. A penchant for simplifying intricate issues.

3. Employing propaganda, media control, or even force to curtail opposition.

4. Cultivating a personal brand interwoven with the nation's destiny.

By understanding these historical trajectories, societies can better equip themselves to recognize and potentially mitigate similar patterns in the unfolding future.

How Past Strongmen Used Media and Public Sentiment to Their Advantage

Throughout history, various strongmen have exhibited astute media mastery, leveraging it to bolster their image, suppress dissent, and influence the masses. This section elucidates the media strategies and manipulation of public sentiment by some of the West's notable leaders, including the controversial figure of Donald Trump.

1. Benito Mussolini (Italy)

Media Mastery: Mussolini's initial career in journalism gave him insights into media's influential nature. By assuming control over newspapers, radio, and film, he curated a consistent pro-fascist narrative.

Shaping Sentiment: By emphasizing national pride, discipline, and Italy's return to its imperial glory days, Mussolini catered to the populace's yearning for stability and direction in the tumultuous post-WWI period.

2. Adolf Hitler (Germany)

Media Mastery: With Joseph Goebbels helming Nazi propaganda, the regime commandeered newspapers, radios, and films. The message was singular: the magnificence of the Reich and the peril of the Jews.

Shaping Sentiment: Orchestrated mass rallies, amplified by media broadcasts, showcased Hitler's oratory prowess, evoking nationalistic sentiments. The Jews, communists, and other groups were conveniently scapegoated, focusing public discontent toward them.

3. Francisco Franco (Spain)

Media Mastery: Franco's regime instituted media censorship, meticulously crafting a narrative that idolized his leadership and vision for Spain.

Shaping Sentiment: By promoting a unified, Catholic Spain, Franco suppressed regional identities. The portrayal of him as the bulwark against communism and chaos ingrained his indispensable position in many Spaniards' minds.

4. António de Oliveira Salazar (Portugal)

Media Mastery: Under Salazar's "Estado Novo," media was censored and streamlined, ensuring a harmonized, regime-friendly narrative.

Shaping Sentiment: Propaganda accentuated Portugal's Catholic heritage and the impending threat of communism, painting Salazar's leadership as a safeguard against socio-political deterioration.

5. Joseph McCarthy (United States)

Media Mastery: McCarthy adeptly utilized television and radio to amplify his anti-communist crusade, casting a wide net of influence.

Shaping Sentiment: Tapping into the Cold War paranoia, McCarthy's allegations of communist infiltration in American institutions resonated with the prevailing fears, embedding "McCarthyism" in American lexicon.

6. Donald Trump (United States)

Media Mastery: Donald Trump, a media-savvy figure, embraced both traditional and digital platforms. His prolific use of Twitter bypassed conventional media, reaching millions directly with unfiltered messages. His contentious relationship with mainstream media, labeling many as "fake news," was a strategic move to discredit criticism and foster distrust.

Shaping Sentiment: Trump's "Make America Great Again" mantra resonated with a segment of the populace disillusioned by globalization, immigration, and perceived elitism. His candid, sometimes abrasive style, coupled with a clear demarcation of allies and "enemies," invigorated his base, creating a fervent and loyal following. His ability to pinpoint societal anxieties and offer straightforward solutions, whether on immigration or economic issues, painted him as a decisive leader in the eyes of many.

Conclusion

The power of media, when harnessed effectively, can shape societal narratives, bolster leaders, and even redefine realities. From Mussolini to Trump, these strongmen capitalized on this power, manipulating public sentiment to fortify their positions. Their strategies underscore the perennial importance of critical thinking and media literacy in any democratic society.

Chapter 4: Modern Media and the Strongman

The Role of Social Media, Echo Chambers, and Misinformation

In the digital age, the dynamics of media and its influence have undergone a seismic shift. The rise of social media platforms, the phenomenon of echo chambers, and the rapid spread of misinformation are among the most impactful changes. This chapter delves into how these elements intertwine, and their significance in the ascent and maintenance of modern-day strongmen.

1. Social Media: A Double-Edged Sword

Instantaneous Outreach: Social media platforms, with their vast user bases, offer politicians an unparalleled avenue to connect with citizens directly. Leaders can communicate policies, achievements, and opinions without the traditional media's mediation. This directness can foster a sense of authenticity and intimacy with the audience.

The Algorithmic Effect: However, the very algorithms that power these platforms also contribute to polarization. By prioritizing content that aligns with users' existing beliefs and preferences, they inadvertently create echo chambers, limiting exposure to diverse viewpoints.

Mobilization & Movements: The power of social media to mobilize is undeniable. From campaign rallies to digital movements, platforms like Twitter, Facebook, and Instagram serve as potent tools for rallying support, galvanizing followers, and even organizing on-ground events.

2. Echo Chambers: The Illusion of Majority

Reinforcing Beliefs: Echo chambers amplify and reinforce individuals' existing beliefs. When users predominantly see content that aligns with their views, it not only strengthens those beliefs but can also lead to the misconception that theirs is the majority or mainstream perspective.

Marginalizing Dissent: Within these digital bubbles, dissenting voices are often drowned out, ridiculed, or outright blocked. This can create an environment where opposing views are not only in the minority but are also perceived as 'wrong' or 'misinformed.'

Polarization and Radicalization: Over time, consistent exposure to extreme views can shift perceptions. Moderate stances may be seen as weak or uninformed, pushing individuals further along the spectrum of beliefs and sometimes leading to radicalization.

3. Misinformation: The Digital Plague

Speed and Spread: False information spreads rapidly on social media. Sensationalized headlines, memes, and videos can go viral within hours, reaching millions. By the time corrections or retractions are made, the damage is often irreparable.

Tapping into Emotions: Misinformation is particularly potent because it often taps into strong emotions — fear, anger, or pride. Such emotionally charged content is more likely to be shared, further accelerating its spread.

Weaponizing Falsehoods: Modern strongmen can capitalize on misinformation, either by disseminating it to discredit opponents or by portraying themselves as the sole purveyors of 'truth' in a world riddled with 'fake news.' This not only bolsters their image but also sows distrust in traditional media and institutions.

4. Strongmen in the Digital Era

Crafting Narratives: With the tools and tactics available in the digital realm, strongmen can craft and control narratives like never before. They can highlight their achievements, downplay criticisms, and set the public discourse's tone and direction.

Digital Populism: Many modern strongmen use social media to champion populist causes, positioning themselves as the voice of the 'common man' against the 'elite.' This digital populism, fueled by real-time feedback and engagement metrics, allows them to adapt and refine their message continuously.

Bypassing Gatekeepers: Traditional media, once the gatekeepers of information, find their roles diminished. Strongmen can bypass them, reaching their audience directly through tweets, live streams, and posts. Any critical coverage can be swiftly labeled as bias or 'fake news,' further eroding public trust in traditional sources.

Conclusion

The interplay of social media, echo chambers, and misinformation paints a complex picture of the modern media landscape. While these platforms have democratized content creation and dissemination, they've also given rise to challenges that democracies around the world grapple with. For strongmen, these digital avenues offer both opportunities and obstacles. Navigating this realm effectively can mean the difference between fleeting relevance and enduring influence. As we continue to integrate digital platforms into our daily lives, understanding their power and pitfalls becomes paramount for a well-informed, cohesive society.

How Strongmen Exploit These Tools to Present Themselves as the Sole Solution

Within the intricate web of modern media, defined by its immediacy and virality, strongmen have identified unique ways to harness its power. By exploiting social media platforms, echo chambers, and misinformation, they adeptly present themselves as not just a solution, but the sole remedy to a nation's problems. This chapter aims to delineate the strategies that these leaders employ to consolidate their image and authority.

1. Direct Engagement with Followers

Personalized Communication: Strongmen often cultivate a persona that transcends their political role, positioning themselves as 'one of the people.' Using platforms like Twitter or Instagram, they share personal moments, opinions, and narratives, establishing a quasi-personal relationship with followers.

Real-time Feedback Loop: The instantaneous nature of feedback on social media allows strongmen to gauge public sentiment in real-time, adjusting their messages and tactics accordingly. This dynamic, interactive communication fosters a sense of direct dialogue, as if the leader is in perpetual conversation with the citizenry.

2. Establishing a 'Them vs. Us' Dichotomy

Identifying Common Enemies: Strongmen often harness digital platforms to identify or amplify perceived threats – whether they are political rivals, foreign entities, or certain societal groups. By consistently highlighting these 'enemies,' they can rally their base around a shared opposition.

Presenting Themselves as Saviors: Against the backdrop of these constructed threats, strongmen deftly position themselves as the nation's sole protectors. They emphasize the unique qualities, knowledge, or destiny that ostensibly equips them to fend off these dangers, further embedding their indispensability in the public psyche.

3. Controlling and Manipulating Information

Spreading Favorable Narratives: By fostering close ties with friendly media outlets or directly controlling them, strongmen ensure a steady flow of positive coverage. They amplify achievements, however minor, while deflecting or suppressing criticisms.

Discrediting Unfavorable Sources: Labels such as 'fake news' or 'biased media' become handy tools. By consistently casting doubt on the credibility of critical voices, strongmen attempt to make their narratives the only trustworthy ones.

Misinformation as a Weapon: Sometimes, the spread of false or misleading information isn't just a byproduct of the digital age; it's a calculated strategy. Whether it's false claims about political rivals or misleading statistics that bolster their agendas, strongmen and their allies can utilize misinformation to muddy waters and shape perceptions.

4. Amplifying Echo Chambers

Promotion of Sympathetic Voices: Within the vast digital landscape, strongmen often spotlight and promote voices that align with their views. This can range from retweeting supportive individuals to granting exclusive interviews to friendly digital influencers.

Silencing or Marginalizing Dissent: Through both overt and covert methods, strongmen work to silence dissenting voices. This might manifest as online harassment campaigns against critics, legal actions against detractors, or the promotion of alternative narratives that drown out opposition.

5. Constructing a Persona of Strength and Decisiveness

Showcasing Bold Actions: The digital realm, with its penchant for virality, is the perfect stage for strongmen to showcase their 'bold' decisions. Whether it's a drastic policy move or a confrontational speech, these actions, when amplified online, fortify their image as decisive leaders unafraid of consequences.

Emphasizing Simplicity in Complexity: In an age of information overload, many people yearn for simplicity. Strongmen often reduce complex issues to digestible, binary choices. By presenting problems and their solutions in clear-cut terms, they appeal to those overwhelmed by the intricacies of modern challenges.

Conclusion

In leveraging the tools and tendencies of the digital age, modern strongmen have refined age-old tactics of persuasion, control, and dominance. By intertwining their narratives with the algorithms and echo chambers of the online world, they've managed to amplify their reach and resonance. Recognizing these strategies is the first step in fostering a media landscape that champions truth, diversity, and constructive dialogue over division and deceit.

The "Us vs. Them" Narrative and the Polarization of Modern Media

The "Us vs. Them" narrative is far from new. Historically, leaders, tribes, and nations have leveraged this dichotomy to unify groups against perceived threats. However, in the age of digital media, this age-old tactic has gained new potency, intricacy, and reach. The modern media landscape, characterized by instant communication, selective algorithms, and echo chambers, is fertile ground for the spread of such binary narratives. In this chapter, we'll explore the dynamics of this polarization and its implications in the context of modern strongmen.

1. The Roots of the Dichotomy

Psychological Origins: Humans, by nature, categorize. It's a cognitive shortcut, helping us make sense of the world. This instinct to group and label – friends or foes, insiders or outsiders – is deeply embedded in our psyche. Modern media simply amplifies and exploits this tendency.

Social Cohesion: Historically, rallying against a common enemy or threat has been an effective way to build social cohesion. By identifying an "other," leaders can consolidate support and foster unity within their in-group.

2. Digital Media: The Perfect Amplifier

Algorithmic Biases: Social media platforms are designed to keep users engaged. To achieve this, algorithms often prioritize content that aligns with users' existing beliefs, leading to the creation of digital echo chambers where opposing views are rare.

Rapid Spread: The speed at which information (or misinformation) spreads on digital platforms can quickly solidify the "Us vs. Them" narrative. A single tweet, video, or meme can go viral in hours, reaching global audiences.

Anonymous Interactions: Online anonymity or the veil of digital interaction can embolden extreme views. Without face-to-face accountability, divisive rhetoric can flourish.

3. Strongmen and the Binary Narrative

Simplifying Complex Issues: The "Us vs. Them" narrative offers a simplification of often complex socio-political issues. Instead of nuanced discussions, strongmen can reduce debates to binary choices, which can be more palatable for mass consumption.

Mobilizing Support: By positioning themselves as the defenders of "Us" against the threat of "Them," strongmen can rally and mobilize their base. This dynamic can foster fierce loyalty, as supporters often feel they're engaged in a battle for their way of life.

Deflecting Criticism: This narrative also serves as a shield. Critics or dissenting voices can be quickly labeled as part of "Them," effectively discrediting them in the eyes of loyal supporters.

4. Implications for Society and Democracy

Eroding Middle Ground: As media becomes more polarized, the middle ground, where compromise and dialogue occur, starts eroding. This can lead to a fragmented society, where reconciliation becomes challenging.

Rise of Populism: The "Us vs. Them" narrative often dovetails with populist rhetoric, which pits the "common people" against the "corrupt elite." This can lead to the rise and consolidation of populist leaders who claim to represent the true voice of the masses.

Undermining Institutions: In the process of establishing a clear enemy, strongmen might target longstanding institutions – the media, judiciary, or academia. Over time, this can undermine public trust in these vital pillars of democracy.

5. Breaking the Cycle

Promoting Media Literacy: Educating citizens about the workings and biases of digital media can be a significant step. A media-literate populace can better navigate the information landscape, discerning fact from fiction.

Fostering Dialogue: Initiatives that promote inter-group dialogue can help bridge divides. Whether it's community-driven efforts, workshops, or digital platforms dedicated to constructive debate, creating spaces for open conversation is crucial.

Algorithmic Transparency: Tech companies can play a role by making their content recommendation algorithms more transparent and providing users with more control over their digital feeds.

Conclusion

While the "Us vs. Them" narrative might be an age-old strategy, its manifestation in the digital age poses unique challenges to societal cohesion and democratic values. Recognizing its mechanics and implications is the first step towards countering its divisive pull. As we grapple with the realities of our interconnected world, finding ways to foster unity and understanding becomes not just a noble pursuit, but a vital one.

Chapter 5: Economic Disparity and the Promise of Redemption

The Widening Gap Between the Rich and the Poor in the West

The economic disparity between the rich and the poor, often encapsulated in the phrase "income inequality," has been a growing concern in Western nations. This gap isn't just a matter of numbers; it has tangible implications on social cohesion, political stability, and even the foundational ideals of Western democracies. In this chapter, we'll dive into the roots, ramifications, and the role of strongmen in this complex economic narrative.

1. The Historical Context

Post-World War Boom: The decades following World War II saw significant economic growth and relatively low levels of income inequality in many Western nations. The "golden age" was characterized by high taxes on the wealthy, strong labor unions, and robust public investment.

Economic Shifts in the Late 20th Century: As the 20th century neared its close, several factors, including globalization, technological advancement, and political shifts, began to reshape the Western economic landscape. The rise of neoliberal policies, favoring deregulation and tax cuts, particularly benefited the wealthy and the corporations.

2. The Current Landscape

Stagnating Wages: While productivity has risen in many Western countries, wages, particularly for those at the bottom, have stagnated. The benefits of economic growth have disproportionately flowed to the top, leading to widening wealth disparities.

Diminishing Social Mobility: Once hailed as the lands of opportunity, many Western nations now grapple with diminishing social mobility. The chances of someone born in the lower economic quintile reaching the top have dwindled over the decades.

Concentration of Wealth: Today, a significant portion of wealth in the West is concentrated in the hands of a tiny elite. Reports highlighting that a handful of billionaires possess wealth equivalent to that of the bottom half of the population have become emblematic of this disparity.

3. Societal and Political Implications

Eroding Trust in Institutions: As the gap widens, faith in institutions, from governments to financial systems, erodes. Many perceive these entities as being captured by the elite, furthering their interests at the expense of the majority.

Rise in Populism: Economic disparity often fuels populist sentiments. Leaders championing the cause of "the people" against the "corrupt elite" find a receptive audience among those feeling left behind by the modern economic order.

Social Strains: Beyond economics, income inequality exacerbates social issues. Disparities in health, education, and even life expectancy between the rich and the poor have become more pronounced.

4. Strongmen and the Promise of Redemption

Capitalizing on Discontent: Many strongmen leaders tap into the economic anxieties of the masses. By portraying themselves as champions of the "forgotten" or "ignored," they cultivate a base of passionate supporters.

Promising Simple Solutions: The allure of strongmen, in part, lies in their promise of straightforward solutions to complex economic woes. Whether it's pledging to bring back lost jobs, imposing tariffs, or cutting down on immigration, these solutions often appeal to those yearning for economic redemption.

Manipulating the Narrative: While some strongmen genuinely aim to address economic disparities, others might merely use the narrative as a means to power. Once in office, their policies might not necessarily align with their populist rhetoric.

5. Addressing the Gap: Potential Pathways

Progressive Taxation: Instituting a more progressive tax system can help redistribute wealth and fund public services that benefit the broader population.

Strengthening Labor: Reinvigorating labor movements and ensuring workers' rights can lead to better wages and working conditions, helping bridge some of the economic divides.

Investing in Education: Ensuring access to quality education for all, irrespective of their economic background, is a long-term strategy to enhance social mobility and reduce income disparities.

Reigning in Corporate Power: Implementing regulations that check the unchecked power of mega-corporations can prevent wealth concentration and ensure a more equitable economic landscape.

Conclusion

The widening gap between the rich and the poor in the West isn't merely an economic statistic; it's a reflection of societal values, political priorities, and the very nature of modern democracies. As this chasm grows, the allure of strongmen promising redemption becomes more potent. Understanding the roots and ramifications of this disparity is crucial, not just to address the economic imbalances but to safeguard the democratic ideals that the West cherishes.

Strongmen's Promises of Economic Revival and Stability

Strongmen leaders often rise to power on a tide of public discontent. One of the most compelling sources of such discontent is economic disparity and instability. By offering promises of economic revival and a return to a perceived golden era, strongmen appeal to those who feel left behind by globalization, technological change, and shifting economic tides. In this chapter, we'll explore the economic rhetoric of strongmen, the allure of their promises, and the realities behind their proclamations.

1. The Rhetoric of Restoration

Nostalgia for a Bygone Era: Strongmen often evoke memories of a nation's past economic glory, promising a return to times when jobs were plentiful, and national industries thrived. This evocation of nostalgia serves as a potent tool to galvanize support, especially among older generations.

Blame and Responsibility: Part of the strongman's appeal lies in identifying culprits for current economic woes, be it global institutions, foreign competitors, immigrants, or the "corrupt elite." By providing clear adversaries, strongmen simplify complex economic narratives.

2. Promises of Direct Action

Protectionism: Many strongmen advocate for protectionist policies, including tariffs and trade barriers, as solutions to domestic economic challenges. By doing so, they claim to protect national industries from foreign competition and safeguard local jobs.

Infrastructure Development: Grand projects, from building walls to constructing mega-infrastructure, are often touted as tangible evidence of a strongman's commitment to national progress and job creation.

Support for Traditional Industries: Whether it's coal mining, manufacturing, or agriculture, strongmen often pledge support for sectors that have faced challenges in recent times, portraying themselves as champions of the "common worker."

3. The Allure of Stability

Certainty in Uncertain Times: In an era marked by rapid change and uncertainty, the strongman's promise of stability and order can be highly attractive. Their authoritarian style, characterized by decisiveness and often a disdain for bureaucratic processes, gives an impression of efficiency.

Control over Economic Forces: The strongman often claims an ability to control and steer economic forces in ways that traditional politicians cannot. This includes direct negotiations with corporations, making high-profile deals, or exerting pressure on businesses to align with national interests.

4. The Reality Behind the Rhetoric

Short-Term Gains vs. Long-Term Implications: While some policies may yield immediate results or create a facade of economic progress, they often carry long-term implications. For instance, protectionist measures might save jobs in one sector but can lead to price increases or trade wars that harm the economy in the long run.

Populist Measures with Hidden Costs: Initiatives like infrastructure projects can boost employment and stimulate the economy. However, without proper oversight and transparency, they can also lead to corruption, ballooning national debts, and projects that serve more as political symbols than actual economic assets.

Selective Economic Narratives: The strongman's narrative often highlights success stories while downplaying or ignoring failures. This selective storytelling can create a distorted image of economic progress.

5. The Risks of Centralized Economic Control

Vulnerability to Mismanagement: Centralized control, especially when it bypasses institutional checks and balances, is vulnerable to mismanagement. Economic decisions made for political reasons can have detrimental effects on the national economy.

Dependency and Patronage: A strongman's economy can lead to a system of patronage, where businesses and industries are beholden to the leader for favors, subsidies, or licenses. This can stifle competition, innovation, and meritocracy.

Economic Retaliation: Policies that antagonize international partners can lead to economic retaliation, be it in the form of sanctions, tariffs, or reduced foreign investments. Such isolation can harm the national economy, particularly in our interconnected globalized world.

Conclusion

Strongmen's promises of economic revival and stability resonate deeply with segments of the population disillusioned with the status quo. While some of their strategies might yield short-term gains, it's crucial to evaluate them in the broader context of long-term sustainability, global economic realities, and the principles of open and competitive economies. In the interplay between populist rhetoric and complex economic dynamics, discerning substance from spectacle is both a challenge and a necessity.

Real vs. Perceived Economic Threats and Their Implications

The line between reality and perception is often blurred in the realm of economic threats, especially in an era dominated by sensationalist media and strongman rhetoric. Differentiating between genuine economic challenges and those that are magnified or distorted for political gain is critical for understanding the socio-political dynamics of the West. In this section, we'll explore the interplay between real and perceived economic threats and delve into their implications for society, politics, and the allure of strongmen leaders.

1. Real Economic Threats

Technological Disruption: The rapid pace of technological advancement has disrupted traditional industries. Automation, for instance, threatens jobs in sectors ranging from manufacturing to customer service.

Globalization: While globalization has many benefits, it has also led to the offshoring of jobs and increased competition from abroad. Domestic industries, especially those unable to adapt quickly, face significant challenges.

Economic Cycles: Economic downturns, recessions, and financial crises are tangible threats that have immediate and often severe implications for employment, investment, and overall economic health.

Environmental Concerns: Climate change and environmental degradation pose long-term threats to economies, especially those heavily reliant on industries like agriculture or coastal tourism.

2. Perceived Economic Threats

Immigration: While immigrants often contribute significantly to economies by filling labor gaps and paying taxes, they are sometimes perceived as job stealers or as burdens on social welfare systems.

Foreign Competition: Foreign competitors are often blamed for economic woes, even when domestic factors or technological changes are more significant contributors to industry challenges.

Global Institutions: Entities like the World Trade Organization or the International Monetary Fund are sometimes seen as imposing unfavorable conditions on nations, even if their roles are more nuanced.

Cultural Shifts: Changes in societal values, often driven by younger generations or influenced by global trends, can be perceived as threats to traditional economic structures, even if they don't have direct economic implications.

3. The Role of Media and Misinformation

Echo Chambers: The rise of social media and algorithm-driven content has created echo chambers where individuals are often exposed only to information that aligns with their pre-existing beliefs, magnifying perceived threats.

Sensationalism: Media outlets, aiming to capture audience attention, might amplify certain economic issues while downplaying others, skewing public perception.

Misinformation and Fake News: The spread of false information can exacerbate perceptions of economic threats, leading to unwarranted fears or misguided solutions.

4. Strongmen and the Manipulation of Perception

Capitalizing on Fears: Strongmen leaders often tap into perceived economic threats, amplifying them to galvanize support. By positioning themselves as the solution to these threats, they cultivate loyalty and justify their authoritarian approaches.

Diversion Tactics: By magnifying certain issues, strongmen can divert attention from other challenges, whether they're political scandals, policy failures, or genuine economic threats they're ill-equipped to handle.

Simplifying Complexities: A hallmark of strongman rhetoric is the simplification of complex economic narratives. By offering clear enemies and straightforward solutions, they appeal to those overwhelmed by the intricacies of modern economies.

5. Implications for Societies and Democracies

Policy Missteps: Policies based on perceived threats rather than real challenges can be misguided, leading to economic inefficiencies, missed opportunities, or even crises.

Social Fragmentation: Disparities between reality and perception can lead to societal divides, with different segments of the population having starkly different understandings of economic realities.

Erosion of Trust: When the public realizes that certain threats have been exaggerated or manipulated, it can lead to an erosion of trust in leadership, institutions, and even the media.

Democracy at Risk: Democracies thrive on informed electorates. When perceptions are heavily skewed, electoral decisions might not reflect the best interests of the public, posing risks to the very fabric of democratic systems.

Conclusion

Differentiating between real and perceived economic threats is more than an academic exercise; it's fundamental to the health of economies, societies, and democracies. As the West grapples with a rapidly changing economic landscape, understanding these dynamics becomes essential to navigate challenges and harness opportunities effectively. Moreover, it's a crucial defense against the potential manipulations of strongman leaders or any entities aiming to exploit public perceptions for their ends.

Chapter 6: Identity and Cultural Fears

The Strongman's Play on Cultural Identity and National Pride

In the intricate tapestry of political maneuvering, the threads of cultural identity and national pride hold significant sway. Strongmen, with their characteristic grasp of populist sentiment, deftly weave these elements into their narratives. Their emphasis on restoring or defending cultural values and national honor resonates with many, especially in times of perceived cultural erosion or external threat. In this chapter, we will dissect the strongman's approach to cultural identity and national pride, exploring both its allure and its implications.

1. Nostalgia for a "Golden Era"

Revisiting the Past: Strongmen frequently invoke a nation's past glories, referencing a time when the culture was "pure" and the nation stood tall and unchallenged. This can resonate particularly with older generations who feel the current cultural shifts are eroding traditional values.

The Decline Narrative: Alongside celebrating the past, strongmen paint the present as a time of decline and decay. They emphasize the erosion of traditional values, often blaming external influences, liberal elites, or minority groups for this perceived degradation.

2. Defining the "True" National Identity

Cultural Gatekeeping: Strongmen often position themselves as the defenders of "true" national identity. This involves defining what constitutes genuine cultural practices, beliefs, and values, often excluding diverse and pluralistic elements.

Exclusion and Othering: By setting boundaries on what represents the "authentic" culture, strongmen inherently create an "us vs. them" dichotomy. Minorities, immigrants, or even progressive sections within the country can be portrayed as threats to the established cultural norm.

3. Symbols, Rituals, and Rhetoric

Emphasis on Symbols: Flags, anthems, monuments, and other national symbols become focal points in the strongman's narrative. They're not just celebrated but defended fiercely, with any critique or alternative interpretation seen as a direct assault on national pride.

Ritualistic Celebrations: National holidays, anniversaries, or even newly instituted celebrations can be amplified, serving both as displays of cultural pride and reminders of the strongman's role in upholding these traditions.

Championing Cultural Artefacts: Traditional arts, crafts, music, and dance might receive renewed patronage, being showcased as representations of the pure national essence.

4. The Allure of a Homogeneous Nation

Simplifying Complex Identities: A single, unified national identity can seem appealing, offering clarity in contrast to the muddled, overlapping identities in multicultural societies.

Safety in Familiarity: Especially in times of rapid change or external threats, retreating to familiar cultural norms and values can feel comforting. The strongman promises this return, presenting himself as a bulwark against the forces of change.

5. Implications of Cultural and Nationalist Play

Stifling of Dissent: By intertwining their leadership with the very essence of national identity, strongmen can label dissenters as not just political opponents, but as traitors to the nation.

Erosion of Pluralism: A monolithic interpretation of culture inherently sidelines diverse voices. Over time, this can erode the very pluralism that often enriches societies, leading to a narrower, impoverished cultural landscape.

Increased Polarization: The strong emphasis on a singular identity can deepen rifts within society. Those who align with the strongman's version of culture are pitted against those who don't, leading to societal divisions that can outlast the strongman's tenure.

Potential for Xenophobia: The externalization of threats can lead to heightened suspicions of foreigners, immigrants, or even external cultural influences. This can manifest as xenophobic policies, hate crimes, or general societal hostility towards the "other."

Conclusion

The realm of cultural identity and national pride is deeply emotional, tied to individuals' sense of belonging and self-worth. Strongmen tap into these sentiments, offering a vision of restored honor and defended traditions. While this can create a cohesive in-group, it often comes at the cost of exclusion, division, and a narrowing of cultural horizons. For societies navigating the strongman's narrative, striking a balance between pride in one's heritage and openness to evolving cultural landscapes becomes the critical challenge.

How Migration, Globalization, and Cultural Shifts Amplify Fears

The modern era, characterized by unprecedented mobility, interconnectedness, and change, has brought about numerous benefits, including economic growth, technological advancements, and cultural exchange. However, alongside these advantages, migration, globalization, and cultural shifts have also stirred underlying fears in many. The dynamics of these changes and the anxieties they produce play directly into the hands of strongmen leaders who capitalize on them. Let's delve into how these factors amplify fears and the reasons behind such anxieties.

1. Migration and the Fear of the "Other"

Changing Demographics: As people move across borders seeking better opportunities or escaping conflicts, host countries often experience demographic changes. The influx of different cultures, religions, and languages can be unsettling for some, especially if they perceive their cultural norms as being threatened.

Economic Concerns: Migrants are sometimes perceived as competitors for jobs, housing, and social resources. Even if such fears are statistically unfounded, they can be potent and divisive.

Cultural Homogenization: There's an underlying fear that mass migration might lead to a dilution of the host country's cultural identity, traditions, and values.

2. Globalization and the Loss of Economic Sovereignty

Economic Dependency: Globalization ties economies together. While this can lead to growth, it also means local economies might be affected by events half a world away, leading to a feeling of vulnerability.

Cultural Commodification: With globalization, cultural elements often become commodities. Traditional crafts, practices, or even festivals can be commercialized, leading to fears of cultural erosion.

Influence of Global Institutions: Entities such as the World Trade Organization, International Monetary Fund, and multinational corporations can be perceived as having undue influence on national policies, igniting concerns about a loss of sovereignty.

3. Cultural Shifts and the Challenge to Established Norms

Changing Moral Landscapes: As societies evolve, so do their moral compasses. Changes in views on issues like LGBTQ+ rights, gender roles, and religious practices can be jarring for those who hold traditional views.

Technological Disruption: The digital age has transformed not only how we work but also how we interact, leading to concerns about weakened family ties, eroding social skills, and a loss of privacy.

Inter-generational Differences: Younger generations, growing up in a more interconnected world, often have values and aspirations that differ from their predecessors, leading to inter-generational tensions.

4. The Amplification Mechanism: Media, Politics, and Society

Media Sensationalism: Stories that cater to fears about migration, globalization, or cultural shifts are more likely to get clicks and shares, driving media outlets to prioritize them, thus amplifying concerns.

Political Capital: Politicians, especially those leaning towards populism, recognize the potency of these fears and often stoke them to rally their base.

Societal Echo Chambers: With social media algorithms feeding users content that aligns with their views, misconceptions and fears can be reinforced, creating a feedback loop of anxiety.

5. The Broader Implications of Amplified Fears

Divisive Politics: When fears about identity and culture dominate the political discourse, divisive and exclusionary policies can gain traction.

Missed Opportunities: A society consumed by fear might resist beneficial aspects of migration, globalization, and cultural shifts, such as economic growth, innovation, and cultural enrichment.

Eroded Social Cohesion: Amplified fears can strain societal bonds, leading to mistrust between different community groups and even within them.

Conclusion

Migration, globalization, and cultural shifts are intricate phenomena, each with its set of challenges and opportunities. However, in an atmosphere where these changes are often viewed through a lens of fear, societies risk making decisions based on anxieties rather than facts. While it's essential to address genuine concerns associated with these changes, it's equally crucial to differentiate between grounded fears and those that are inflated, manipulated, or misinformed. Only then can societies navigate the complexities of the modern era with clarity and foresight.

The Promise of a Return to "The Good Old Days"

The allure of nostalgia is potent. Throughout history, societies have often looked back wistfully to a time when things seemed simpler, values were purportedly stronger, and problems, at least in memory, seemed less pervasive. Strongmen, understanding this human tendency, frequently promise a return to these "good old days" as a central component of their campaigns. Let's dive into the appeal of this promise, its implications, and the reality behind such aspirations.

1. The Psychology of Nostalgia

Rose-Tinted Glasses: Our brains are wired to remember positive experiences more vividly than negative ones. Over time, this can lead to an idealized view of the past, where challenges are downplayed, and virtues are exaggerated.

A Simpler Time: In the face of rapid technological and societal changes, the past can appear more straightforward and less daunting, even if this wasn't necessarily the case.

Shared Cultural Memories: Collective memories of a nation's "golden era" can serve as bonding agents, creating a shared sense of identity and purpose.

2. Strongmen and the Nostalgic Narrative

Highlighting Decline: By emphasizing the purported decline in values, safety, and prosperity, strongmen can paint a bleak picture of the present, making the past appear even more appealing.

The Savior Archetype: Once the present is painted as degraded, the strongman positions himself as the savior who can restore past glory, tapping into deep-seated desires for stability and pride.

Selective Memory: In their portrayal of the "good old days," strongmen often omit issues like systemic discrimination, economic disparity, or societal repression, offering a sanitized version of the past.

3. The Societal Appeal

Cultural Anchors: In rapidly changing environments, symbols and narratives from the past serve as anchors, offering a sense of stability and continuity.

Mourning Lost Communities: The nostalgia narrative resonates especially with communities feeling left behind by globalization or societal shifts. The promise of a return offers hope and validation.

Defensive Reaction: For some, rapid cultural changes, be they due to migration, technological advancement, or changing societal norms, can be unsettling. The promise of a return acts as a defensive response against perceived threats.

4. The Challenges and Contradictions

Unattainable Aspirations: The past, in all its complexity, cannot be recreated verbatim. Efforts to do so can lead to regressive policies, which may not address current challenges effectively.

Overlooking Present Advancements: While the past had its merits, the present often offers advancements in areas like technology, medicine, and societal rights. A blind return risks forfeiting these gains.

Potential for Repression: Efforts to revert to past norms can lead to the repression of groups who have only recently gained rights or recognition, deepening societal divides.

5. The Reality Behind the Nostalgia

Were Things Really Better?: While certain aspects might have been better in the past, a holistic view often reveals a mixed bag. For instance, while community bonds might have been stronger, issues like healthcare, civil rights, or economic opportunities might not have been as advanced.

Selective Global Comparisons: Strongmen, while promising a return to past glory, often overlook the fact that other nations too have their nostalgic eras. Is the aspiration then to revert to a time when the nation was globally dominant? If so, this overlooks the interconnectedness of the modern world.

Evolving Challenges: The problems faced by societies evolve. While a return to past strategies might address older issues, they might not be equipped to tackle contemporary challenges.

Conclusion

The allure of "the good old days" is undeniable. However, it's crucial for societies to differentiate between the comforting glow of nostalgia and the practical realities of governance. While lessons from the past are invaluable, a mere reversion, as opposed to evolution, might not serve the best interests of a nation. As societies navigate the promises of strongmen, a balanced understanding of the past, an appreciation of the present, and a clear-eyed vision for the future are essential.

Chapter 7: Institutions Under Siege

How Strongmen Challenge Democratic Institutions

Democratic institutions, ranging from the free press to the judiciary, play an integral role in ensuring checks and balances within a democracy. These institutions work to safeguard individual freedoms, uphold the rule of law, and prevent the consolidation of power. Strongmen, however, often perceive these institutions as barriers to their agendas. This chapter explores the various strategies employed by strongmen to challenge, undermine, or repurpose democratic institutions to consolidate their hold on power.

1. Discrediting the Free Press

Labeling as "Fake News": One of the primary tactics employed by strongmen is to discredit unfavorable news outlets by labeling them as purveyors of "fake news." This serves to sow doubt among the public and delegitimize critical reporting.

Direct Suppression: In more extreme cases, strongmen might shut down media houses, imprison journalists, or employ state resources to control media narratives.

Promotion of State Media: To counter independent journalism, strongmen might bolster state-owned media outlets, turning them into propaganda machines that amplify their narratives.

2. Undermining the Judiciary

Packing the Courts: Strongmen often attempt to fill courts, especially higher courts, with loyalists who might be more inclined to support their actions, even if they challenge constitutional norms.

Discrediting Unfavorable Rulings: When courts rule against their interests, strongmen may resort to public campaigns that malign the judiciary, presenting it as biased or out of touch with the "real" will of the people.

Legal Overhauls: In some instances, strongmen push for legal reforms under the guise of efficiency or modernization but with the real intent of centralizing judicial power.

3. Manipulating Electoral Systems

Gerrymandering: Redrawing electoral districts to favor a specific party or demographic is a common tactic employed to ensure electoral victories.

Voter Suppression: By enacting strict voter ID laws, limiting early voting, or closing down polling stations in strategic areas, strongmen can disproportionately affect voter turnout in regions less supportive of their reign.

Control of Electoral Commissions: Dominating or influencing electoral commissions can provide strongmen with the tools to manipulate election results subtly.

4. Curbing Civil Liberties

Suppressing Protests: Strongmen often frame protests and civil unrest as threats to national security, justifying excessive force, curfews, or other restrictive measures.

Legislating Against Freedoms: Under the guise of national interest, laws might be introduced that limit freedom of assembly, expression, or association. These laws can be selectively enforced to curb opposition.

Surveillance State: The establishment of extensive surveillance mechanisms can deter dissent, with the public becoming wary of state eavesdropping and potential repercussions.

5. Co-opting or Side-lining Opponents

Bribery and Patronage: To ensure loyalty, strongmen might offer lucrative government contracts, positions, or other perks to potential opponents, effectively co-opting them.

Character Assassination: Those who remain vocal against strongmen might find themselves at the center of smear campaigns, aimed at tarnishing their reputation and undermining their credibility.

Legal Prosecution: Opposition figures might face legal challenges, often on trumped-up charges, leading to their imprisonment or disqualification from holding office.

6. Eroding Checks and Balances

Weakening Legislative Bodies: By securing overwhelming majorities or manipulating legislative procedures, strongmen can render parliaments or congresses ineffective as checking bodies.

Centralizing Power: Executive orders, emergency decrees, or the creation of parallel power structures can allow strongmen to bypass traditional checks and balances, consolidating power in their hands.

Undermining Decentralization: Local governance bodies, if perceived as threats, might be stripped of powers, ensuring that decision-making remains centralized.

Conclusion

Democratic institutions, by design, function as bulwarks against the excessive accumulation of power. However, when strongmen decide to challenge these very foundations, democracies find themselves at a crossroads. The resilience of democratic structures depends not only on the robustness of its institutions but also on the vigilance of its citizenry. Recognizing the strategies employed by strongmen to undermine democracy is the first step in mounting an effective defense against such maneuvers. As history has repeatedly shown, the erosion of democratic institutions often paves the way for authoritarianism, making their defense paramount for those valuing democratic ideals.

The Undermining of Checks and Balances

The principle of checks and balances is foundational to democracies. It ensures that no single branch of government — be it the executive, legislative, or judiciary — can amass unchecked power, thereby protecting the rights of citizens and preventing autocratic rule. However, this balance is delicate, and throughout history, strongmen and authoritarian figures have found ways to erode these mechanisms. This chapter delves into the methods employed by these leaders to undermine checks and balances and the consequences such actions have for democratic governance.

1. Concentration of Executive Power

Bypassing Legislation: Strongmen often seek to bypass legislative processes by utilizing executive orders, emergency decrees, or other mechanisms that don't require parliamentary approval.

Creating Parallel Structures: By establishing alternate institutions or bodies loyal to them, strongmen can redirect power and decision-making away from traditional institutions.

Co-opting the Legislative Process: Through intimidation, patronage, or outright manipulation, strongmen might ensure a subservient majority in legislative bodies that rubber-stamp their decisions.

2. Eroding the Independence of the Judiciary

Appointing Loyalists: A judiciary packed with loyalists can serve the dual purpose of legitimizing the strongman's actions and stifling opposition through legal means.

Public Discreditation: Strongmen frequently attempt to undermine trust in the judiciary by painting it as corrupt, elite, or disconnected from the real needs of the people.

Limiting Judicial Review: By placing constraints on the judiciary's ability to review executive actions or legislation, strongmen can act with increased impunity.

3. Controlling Information Flow

State Media Monopoly: Controlling or influencing major media outlets ensures that the narrative remains favorable to the strongman, while dissenting voices are marginalized or silenced.

Attacking Independent Media: Beyond just discrediting, some strongmen resort to more direct methods such as legal action, imprisonment, or even violence against journalists.

Promoting Propaganda: A constant stream of state-sponsored content can help mold public opinion, making it harder for independent entities to challenge the strongman's narrative.

4. Curtailing Legislative Oversight

Limiting Debates: By restricting the duration or scope of legislative debates, strongmen can stifle opposition and scrutiny.

Diminishing Committee Powers: Legislative committees, which often play a crucial role in examining issues in depth, might find their powers curtailed, reducing their effectiveness as oversight bodies.

Centralizing Decision Making: Concentrating key decision-making powers within a small group or even a single individual can negate the broader legislative body's role.

5. Suppression of Civil Society and Non-Governmental Entities

Restrictive Legislation: Laws that place burdensome requirements on NGOs or civil society groups can effectively hamper their operations, especially if these groups are critical of the regime.

Financial Constraints: By restricting funding, especially from foreign sources, strongmen can financially choke oppositional groups.

Smear Campaigns: Discrediting civil society leaders or organizations by portraying them as unpatriotic, foreign agents, or destabilizers is a tactic frequently employed to erode their influence.

6. Undermining Mechanisms of Accountability

Discrediting Auditors and Ombudsmen: Institutions that audit government actions or serve as watchdogs might be discredited, rendered powerless, or staffed with loyalists.

Limiting Transparency: Strongmen might reduce the transparency of their actions, making it harder for both institutional and public scrutiny to take place.

Retaliatory Actions: Institutions or individuals that attempt to hold the strongman accountable might face repercussions, from legal actions to more direct forms of intimidation.

Conclusion

The undermining of checks and balances poses a grave threat to democratic governance. It paves the way for unchecked power, diminishes the voice of the opposition, and curtails the rights of citizens. The erosion of these mechanisms doesn't typically occur overnight but is a gradual process, often happening under the guise of national interest, efficiency, or reform. As such, the onus is on citizens, civil society, and democratic institutions worldwide to remain vigilant, recognize the signs of erosion, and take proactive measures to safeguard the essential balance that underpins democratic systems. Without these checks and balances, what is touted as democracy might quickly slide into authoritarianism.

The Public's Waning Trust in Institutions and Its Consequences

Trust is the bedrock of any democratic system. It provides the foundation for mutual respect between the governing and the governed, enabling a social contract where citizens consent to laws and leadership in exchange for protection, representation, and the promise of a better society. However, over recent decades, public trust in various institutions — from the media to the judiciary, and from political bodies to financial systems — has significantly eroded in many Western democracies. This chapter sheds light on the reasons behind this declining trust and the consequences it portends for democracy.

1. Causes of Declining Trust

Perceived Corruption and Nepotism: Cases of corruption, nepotism, or the perceived misuse of power can erode confidence in institutions. When people believe that those in positions of power prioritize personal gain over public service, faith dwindles.

Institutional Inefficiency: Prolonged bureaucracy, cumbersome regulations, or perceived incompetence can lead citizens to question an institution's effectiveness.

Economic Inequality: The widening gap between the rich and the poor, coupled with the perception that institutions primarily serve the elite, diminishes trust among marginalized communities.

Partisan Polarization: When institutions appear to be excessively partisan or driven by a particular ideological stance, their universality and neutrality come into question.

Media Fragmentation: The rise of diverse media outlets, often catering to particular ideological biases, has led to competing narratives, fueling distrust in mainstream media and other institutions.

2. Consequences of Diminished Trust

Reduced Civic Participation: When people don't trust institutions, they are less likely to participate in civic activities such as voting, community service, or even obeying laws.

Rise of Populism: A significant fallout of declining institutional trust is the rise of populist leaders who promise to dismantle the "corrupt" system and offer simplistic solutions, often bypassing these very institutions.

Fragmentation of Society: With diminishing trust, societal cohesion suffers. Communities become more insular, adhering to narrow narratives that confirm their biases, leading to greater societal division.

Erosion of Democratic Norms: Trust is essential for the adherence to democratic norms. Without it, there's a weakening of the societal fabric, leading to a rise in autocratic tendencies, disregard for the rule of law, and the undermining of checks and balances.

Economic Implications: Trust in financial and economic institutions is crucial for stability. A lack of trust can lead to reduced investments, capital flight, and economic downturns.

3. The Vicious Cycle of Distrust

Often, distrust creates a self-fulfilling prophecy. When citizens distrust an institution, they might withhold support or resist its mandates. This resistance can hinder the institution's functioning, which in turn provides further evidence to the public of its ineffectiveness, exacerbating the initial distrust.

4. The Role of Disinformation

In today's digital age, the rapid spread of misinformation and disinformation plays a pivotal role in eroding trust. Fake news, conspiracy theories, and manipulated narratives can quickly gain traction, tarnishing the image of institutions.

5. Global Implications

The decline in trust isn't just a domestic concern. As leading democracies grapple with internal trust issues, their global influence wanes. Autocratic regimes might point to these trust issues as evidence of democracy's inherent flaws, thereby justifying their own governance models.

6. Rebuilding Trust: A Way Forward

While the picture seems bleak, it's not irreversible. Steps can be taken to rebuild trust:

- **Transparency and Accountability:** Institutions must prioritize openness, allowing public scrutiny and taking responsibility for mistakes.
- **Public Engagement:** Regular dialogue with citizens, understanding their concerns, and involving them in decision-making processes can bridge the trust gap.
- **Media Literacy:** Educating the public about media literacy can equip them to differentiate between credible sources and misinformation, reducing the impact of fake news.
- **Reforming Institutions:** Addressing inherent flaws, combating corruption, and ensuring institutions truly serve public interests is essential.

Conclusion

The waning public trust in institutions is a clarion call for introspection and reform. Democracy, at its core, relies on the mutual trust between its institutions and its citizens. Addressing the root causes of this distrust, while actively taking measures to rebuild faith, is paramount. If left unchecked, this growing chasm of distrust could very well undermine the foundations of democratic governance, paving the way for instability, division, and the rise of undemocratic forces.

Chapter 8:
The Role of Charisma

The Psychological Appeal of Charismatic Leaders

Charisma, a mysterious allure that captivates and commands attention, has long played a crucial role in leadership. From religious prophets to revolutionary figures, and from corporate moguls to populist politicians, charismatic individuals have historically swayed masses, often invoking fervent devotion. But what drives this psychological appeal? And why do so many individuals fall under the magnetic pull of charismatic leaders, sometimes even against their better judgment?

1. Human Evolution and Leadership

It's helpful to begin by considering the evolutionary perspective. Historically, humans have survived and thrived in groups. Leadership — and the ability to discern effective leaders — became vital for group survival. A leader's charisma might signal confidence, competence, or the promise of a better future. As a result, an innate human predisposition may exist to be drawn to charismatic figures, believing they possess exceptional abilities to navigate challenges.

2. The Need for Meaning and Clarity

One of the most profound psychological appeals of charismatic leaders is their ability to offer clarity in uncertain times. They often present the world in binaries: good vs. evil, us vs. them, right vs. wrong. This simplification provides a clear roadmap for individuals overwhelmed by the complexities of modern life. By adhering to the charismatic leader's vision, followers feel they are part of a larger, meaningful narrative.

3. Emotional Resonance and Validation

Charismatic leaders are adept at resonating with the emotional undercurrents of their audience. They tap into prevalent sentiments, whether it's disillusionment, anger, hope, or fear, and amplify these emotions, making followers feel seen and validated. This emotional connection fosters a strong bond, wherein followers often feel the leader understands them better than they understand themselves.

4. The Halo Effect

Psychologists have identified a cognitive bias known as the "halo effect," where an individual's perceived positive trait in one area leads people to assume they have other positive traits. A charismatic leader might be seen as confident, leading followers to also perceive them as competent, intelligent, or moral, even without concrete evidence.

5. The Promise of Transformation

Charismatic leaders often position themselves as transformative figures, promising not just incremental change but revolutionary shifts. This promise can be particularly seductive to those feeling stuck or disillusioned with the status quo. The idea that a single person can drastically alter the course of their life or society at large offers hope and inspiration.

6. In-group Identity and Collective Effervescence

Charisma often fosters a strong sense of in-group identity. Followers feel they are part of an exclusive club, bound by a shared belief or vision. This collective identity is reinforced at rallies, gatherings, or events, where individuals experience "collective effervescence" — a euphoric energy resulting from being part of a united group.

7. Charisma as a Projection Surface

Often, the appeal of charismatic leaders lies not just in the leaders themselves but in what followers project onto them. These leaders become blank canvases for people's hopes, dreams, and desires. In their charismatic glow, followers see a reflection of who they aspire to be or the world they desire.

8. The Danger of Blind Allegiance

While charisma can inspire and mobilize, it also has a darker side. Over-reliance on a leader's charisma can lead to a suspension of critical thinking. Charismatic leaders, aware of their influence, might exploit this devotion, leading followers down paths not in their best interest. History is rife with examples of charismatic leaders who, buoyed by unchecked adulation, made catastrophic decisions or abused their power.

9. Navigating Charisma in the Modern Age

In an era of mass media and social networks, charisma can be amplified like never before. Leaders can curate their image, reaching followers directly without intermediaries. The potential for charismatic influence (both positive and negative) is thus heightened.

For followers, it's crucial to differentiate between charisma and genuine leadership qualities like competence, integrity, and empathy. While charisma can inspire, it shouldn't be the sole criterion for support or allegiance.

Conclusion

The psychological appeal of charismatic leaders is multifaceted, rooted in evolutionary predispositions, cognitive biases, and deep-seated emotional needs. While charisma can galvanize positive change, unchecked adoration can be perilous. As with all powerful tools, understanding and discernment are essential. In the dance between charismatic leaders and their followers, awareness of the underlying dynamics can lead to more informed, conscious choices.

Techniques and Rhetorical Devices Employed by Strongmen

Charismatic strongmen throughout history have employed a consistent set of techniques and rhetorical devices to captivate their audiences, consolidate power, and further their agendas. These tools, ranging from the linguistic to the performative, not only amplify their charisma but also enable them to navigate the complex socio-political landscapes they seek to dominate. Here, we explore the common strategies employed by strongmen to connect, persuade, and often manipulate their followers.

1. Repetition and Catchphrases

Repeating key phrases and ideas is a classic technique of persuasion. By constantly reinforcing certain concepts, strongmen make their messages memorable and easier to internalize. Over time, these repeated phrases become catchphrases or slogans that serve as rallying cries for their base. They simplify complex issues into digestible sound bites, fostering unity and identification among followers.

2. Simplification and Dichotomies

Strongmen often present issues in stark, binary terms: right vs. wrong, us vs. them, patriot vs. traitor. This simplification reduces the cognitive load on the audience, offering clear-cut solutions to intricate problems. By dividing the world into allies and adversaries, they galvanize support and deflect criticism.

3. Emotional Appeals

Appealing to emotions, rather than reason, is a powerful tool in the strongman's arsenal. Whether stoking fears about perceived threats, invoking nostalgia for a "better past," or inspiring hope for a brighter future, strongmen skillfully manipulate emotional currents to rally supporters.

4. Personal Anecdotes and Relatability

To forge deeper connections with their audience, strongmen often share personal stories or anecdotes. These narratives humanize them, allowing followers to see them as relatable figures who understand their struggles, rather than distant political entities.

5. Ad Hominem Attacks and Mockery

Strongmen frequently resort to personal attacks against opponents, questioning not just their policies but also their character, intelligence, or even appearance. By belittling rivals, they seek to undermine their credibility and elevate themselves in comparison.

6. Myth Creation and the Hero Narrative

A strongman often portrays himself as a singular, heroic figure, chosen to lead the nation through its darkest hours. This self-aggrandizing narrative, which might be rooted in real, exaggerated, or entirely fabricated achievements, strengthens their perceived indispensability.

7. Populist Rhetoric

Populism, with its emphasis on the will of the "common people" against the "corrupt elite," is a favored strategy. Strongmen position themselves as the voice of the silenced majority, promising to topple established systems that have allegedly failed the masses.

8. Rituals and Symbolism

Beyond words, strongmen understand the power of symbols and rituals. From elaborate public ceremonies to the adoption of particular attire or symbols, they create an aura of grandeur and authority. These rituals, steeped in cultural or national significance, often serve to legitimize their rule and connect with collective identity.

9. Controlling the Narrative: Media and Propaganda

Strongmen often exert influence over media, either directly through ownership or indirectly through intimidation and censorship. By controlling the narrative, they can amplify their achievements, suppress dissent, and shape public perception in their favor.

10. The Perpetual Campaign Mode

Even after securing power, many strongmen continue to operate as if they are on the campaign trail. Regular public rallies, speeches, and interactions with the "common people" serve as reminders of their popularity and legitimacy.

11. Victimhood and Persecution Complex

Surprisingly, many strongmen also portray themselves as victims. They claim to be unfairly targeted by the media, the elite, foreign powers, or other perceived enemies. This portrayal not only elicits sympathy but also justifies crackdowns on critics, under the guise of self-defense or national security.

12. Mobilizing the Masses

Strongmen often bypass traditional institutional channels, appealing directly to the masses. By mobilizing public support, they can pressure institutions to align with their objectives or validate their mandates.

Conclusion

The techniques and rhetorical devices employed by strongmen are varied and multifaceted, often tailored to the specific cultural and socio-political context they operate within. However, the underlying principles remain consistent: forge a deep emotional connection, present oneself as the indispensable savior, and neutralize opponents through any means necessary. Understanding these techniques is vital, not just for analyzing political landscapes but also for fostering an informed and discerning electorate. Recognizing manipulation allows individuals and societies to make choices based on reason and values, rather than succumbing to the seductive allure of charismatic strongmen.

Personal Stories, Myths, and the Crafting of a Larger-than-Life Persona

Every charismatic leader, especially strongmen, possesses an uncanny ability to weave personal narratives that resonate deeply with their audience. These stories, often imbued with myths and symbolisms, serve as powerful tools in crafting a larger-than-life persona, allowing the leader to transcend the ordinary and assume an almost mythical stature. But how does this process work, and why is it so effective?

1. Personal Stories as Relatable Narratives

The human brain is hardwired to understand and remember stories. From ancient tales shared around the campfire to modern-day blockbusters, stories shape our perceptions and beliefs. For a strongman, personal stories serve a dual purpose:

- **Relatability**: By sharing tales of humble beginnings, personal struggles, or moments of resilience, strongmen position themselves as 'one of us'. This breaks barriers, making them appear more human and relatable.

- **Inspiration**: These narratives often carry a transformative arc, showcasing the leader's journey from adversity to triumph. Such stories inspire followers, reinforcing the leader's exceptional nature while providing hope for a better future.

2. Myths: Linking the Personal to the Universal

While personal stories resonate on an individual level, myths operate on a universal plane. Myths are timeless tales that, despite their age, remain relevant across generations. When strongmen intertwine their personal narratives with myths, several things happen:

- **Elevation**: Their stories no longer remain mere anecdotes. They are elevated to the realm of legends, making the leader's journey emblematic of a larger human experience.

- **Validation**: By aligning with traditional myths or religious tales, strongmen tap into established belief systems. This not only validates their narratives but also grants them a sacred aura.

- **Archetypes**: Myths are populated by archetypical characters: the hero, the villain, the mentor, the trickster. By positioning themselves as the hero of their mythic narrative, strongmen can easily frame opponents as villains, furthering their agenda.

3. Crafting a Larger-than-Life Persona

A personal narrative intertwined with myth creates a potent mix, laying the groundwork for a larger-than-life persona. However, the crafting of such a persona involves deliberate strategies:

- **Symbolism**: The use of symbols — be it attire, logos, or even personal habits — serves to reinforce the persona. These symbols become synonymous with the leader, evoking specific emotions or beliefs.

- **Rituals**: Public rituals, from elaborate inaugurations to yearly commemorations, serve as reaffirmations of the strongman's stature. They connect the personal with the collective, turning the leader's story into a shared narrative.

- **Controlled Exposure**: While being in the public eye, many strongmen also maintain an air of mystery. Controlled exposure, where the leader is visible but not overly accessible, amplifies intrigue and allure.

- **Choreographed Challenges**: Some strongmen stage or exaggerate challenges, only to overcome them publicly. These 'victories' serve as evidence of their exceptional abilities, further bolstering their persona.

4. The Dangers and Pitfalls

While personal stories and myths are powerful tools, they are not without risks:

- **Overreach**: A narrative that stretches too far from reality can backfire, appearing contrived or inauthentic.
- **Changing Times**: As societies evolve, so do their values and beliefs. A mythic narrative that resonated once might become obsolete or even counterproductive.
- **Belief vs. Reality**: A larger-than-life persona, if believed too deeply by the leader, can lead to hubris. The blurred lines between myth and reality might result in poor decisions or strategic blunders.

Conclusion

The crafting of a larger-than-life persona through personal stories and myths is not mere vanity play. It's a calculated strategy employed by charismatic strongmen to captivate, inspire, and lead. This fusion of the personal and the universal creates leaders who are not just individuals but symbols, embodying the hopes, fears, and aspirations of their followers.

However, the very power of these narratives also makes them dangerous. For followers, it's essential to discern the leader from the legend, appreciating the charisma but remaining vigilant against manipulation. For strongmen, the challenge is to wield their narratives responsibly, ensuring that mythic tales serve the collective good rather than personal aggrandizement.

Chapter 9: Opposition and Resistance

The Range of Responses to Strongmen: From Avid Support to Vehement Resistance

Strongmen leaders, with their larger-than-life personas and polarizing strategies, have always invoked a spectrum of reactions from the populace. From unyielding admiration to fervent opposition, these reactions reveal as much about the society in which these leaders arise as they do about the leaders themselves. Delving into this spectrum, we explore the various factors and underlying sentiments that shape public response to strongmen.

1. Avid Support: The Loyal Base

Strongmen rarely emerge in a vacuum. Their ascent is often facilitated by a significant section of the populace that feels deeply connected to the leader's narrative and promises.

- **Fulfillment of Needs**: Supporters often view strongmen as addressing their unmet needs, be they economic, social, or cultural. The leader is perceived as the solution to systemic problems that other politicians have failed to address.

- **Emotional Connection**: Beyond tangible benefits, many supporters form an emotional bond with the leader. The charisma of the strongman, combined with a compelling narrative, can create a sense of shared identity and purpose.

- **Fear of Alternatives**: For some, support for the strongman stems from fear. Whether it's the threat of external enemies, cultural shifts, or economic decline, the strongman's rhetoric of protection becomes appealing.

2. Conditional Supporters: The Wait-and-See Group

Not all who back a strongman are unwavering in their support. A segment of the populace may support conditionally, often driven by pragmatism.

- **Economic Motivations**: This group might rally behind the strongman in the hope of economic benefits, such as job opportunities or improved business climates.
- **Strategic Alignments**: Some may align with the strongman due to shared short-term goals or mutual adversaries, even if they don't necessarily endorse all of his policies or methods.
- **Desire for Stability**: In turbulent times, a strongman's promise of order and stability can attract those weary of chaos, even if they harbor reservations about the leader's approach.

3. Passive Observers: The Silent Majority

Often overlooked, a sizable portion of the populace might neither ardently support nor actively oppose the strongman. Their reasons can vary:

- **Information Overload**: In the modern age of information, discerning fact from fiction becomes challenging. This group might adopt a wait-and-see approach, hoping for clearer indications of the leader's intentions and outcomes.
- **Fear of Repercussions**: In regimes where dissent is stifled, many prefer to remain silent, avoiding potential consequences of vocal opposition.
- **Apathy or Disillusionment**: Some might be disillusioned with politics altogether, seeing little difference between the strongman and his opponents or feeling that their voice won't make a difference.

4. Vehement Resistance: The Vocal Opposition

Strongmen, with their divisive tactics, invariably face significant opposition. This resistance, often passionate and organized, emerges for various reasons:

- **Ideological Differences**: Many oppose strongmen on ideological grounds, viewing their policies as regressive, authoritarian, or detrimental to democratic values.

- **Protection of Institutions**: Those with a deep commitment to democratic institutions might resist the strongman's attempts to undermine checks and balances.

- **Personal and Group Threats**: Communities or individuals who feel directly threatened by the strongman's rhetoric or policies—be it due to their ethnicity, religion, or political beliefs—often become staunch opponents.

- **Moral and Ethical Grounds**: For some, opposing the strongman is a moral imperative. They perceive the leader's tactics, especially if they involve curbing freedoms or endorsing violence, as fundamentally wrong.

5. International Responses

Beyond domestic reactions, strongmen also elicit varied responses on the international stage:

- **Alliances and Adversaries**: Some nations, based on strategic interests, might align with or oppose the strongman. These alliances can bolster the leader's position domestically, offering external validation.

- **Human Rights Concerns**: International organizations and countries might decry the strongman's actions, especially if they infringe upon human rights or international law.

Conclusion

The range of responses to strongmen is a testament to the complexities of human societies and the multifaceted nature of politics. While strongmen might project an image of unilateral support or opposition, the reality is far more nuanced. Understanding this spectrum is crucial, not only for those who aim to counteract or support such leaders but for anyone striving to grasp the intricate dynamics of political leadership in the modern era.

Success Stories: When and How Democracies Have Checked Strongman Tendencies

The essence of democracy lies in its inbuilt mechanisms of checks and balances, and its core promise to uphold the rule of law, and give voice to its people. Across various moments in history, democracies have been challenged by leaders with strongman tendencies, who've often sought to consolidate their power at the expense of these democratic principles. Yet, the intrinsic strength of many democratic systems has been their ability to resist and counterbalance these tendencies. This exploration takes us through some remarkable instances where democratic forces have risen to the challenge.

1. The United States: The Trump Era and Impeachment Proceedings

The presidency of Donald Trump, from 2017 to 2021, was marked by deep political polarization, with allegations of undermining institutions, sidestepping norms, and polarizing rhetoric.

- **Media Vigilance**: The media played a crucial role in holding the administration accountable. Investigative stories from leading publications shed light on various controversies, ranging from Russian interference in the 2016 election to the Ukraine scandal.

- **Impeachment Proceedings**: Trump faced impeachment twice by the House of Representatives. The first, in December 2019, charged him with abuse of power and obstruction of Congress related to the Ukraine scandal. The second, in January 2021, accused him of incitement of insurrection after the U.S. Capitol riot.

- **Judiciary's Role**: Multiple court decisions, including those from the Supreme Court, upheld the rule of law by checking some of Trump's executive actions, such as the travel ban and diverting funds for a border wall.

- **Electoral Integrity**: Despite allegations of election fraud in the 2020 presidential election, state officials, courts, and the Department of Justice found no widespread fraud, upholding the integrity of the electoral process.

2. Chile: The End of Pinochet's Rule

Under General Augusto Pinochet's reign (1973-1990), Chile grappled with human rights abuses and opposition suppression. But democratic aspirations eventually triumphed.

- **Persistent Opposition**: Throughout Pinochet's rule, various groups opposed his dictatorship, bravely advocating for democracy.
- **1988 Plebiscite**: A 1988 plebiscite determined Pinochet's fate, with a "No" vote signaling an end to his reign.
- **Transition to Democracy**: By 1990, Chile successfully transitioned to a democratic government, marking a return to its democratic traditions.

3. India: The Emergency Era

From 1975 to 1977, Prime Minister Indira Gandhi declared an emergency, curbing civil liberties.

- **Media Dissent**: Despite stringent censorship, outlets like *The Indian Express* voiced their dissent through silent protests, such as publishing blank editorial columns.
- **Grassroots Mobilization**: Leaders like Jayaprakash Narayan rallied citizens against autocratic moves.
- **Electoral Response**: The 1977 elections saw Gandhi's party lose, reflecting public disapproval of the emergency.

4. Turkey: 2017's Power Consolidation Attempt

President Recep Tayyip Erdoğan's 2017 bid to expand presidential powers via a referendum witnessed notable resistance.

- **Vocal Opposition**: Opposition parties vociferously campaigned against the proposed changes.

- **International Oversight**: Observers pointed out irregularities, backing opposition contentions.
- **Civil Society Activism**: NGOs educated the public about potential risks to democratic checks and balances.

5. Gambia: The End of Yahya Jammeh's Rule

After 22 years in power, President Yahya Jammeh was ousted in 2016, exemplifying the triumph of democratic tenets.

- **Regional Diplomacy**: ECOWAS (Economic Community of West African States) intervened diplomatically, and militarily if required, to ensure a smooth transition of power.
- **Public Solidarity**: Widespread support for the newly-elected president, Adama Barrow, signaled the nation's desire for change.
- **Peaceful Transition**: Facing limited domestic support and regional pressure, Jammeh opted for exile, avoiding potential conflict.

Conclusion

These instances underline that even when democracies face challenges from within, their foundational principles, combined with the active participation of civil society, media, judiciary, and the public at large, can counterbalance threats. They stand testament to the enduring spirit of democracy, its resilience, and its capacity for self-correction.

The Importance of a Unified, Compelling Counter-Narrative

In a world saturated with information, narratives have never been more influential. The stories that resonate most are those that evoke emotion, provide clarity, and simplify complexities. Strongmen, with their larger-than-life personas, have a knack for crafting captivating narratives that tap into the sentiments of the masses. In this landscape, for the opposition to effectively challenge these strongmen, it isn't sufficient to merely point out their fallacies. Instead, a compelling, unified counter-narrative is essential. Let's delve into why such a counter-narrative is pivotal and how it can shape the trajectory of resistance.

1. Cutting Through the Noise

Strongmen often dominate media landscapes, either through direct control, intimidation, or their sheer ability to generate headlines. Against this backdrop, dissenting voices can be easily drowned out. A unified counter-narrative, however, has the potency to cut through this noise. By presenting a clear, cohesive alternative, it can gain traction and provide a beacon for those disenchanted with the status quo.

2. Mobilizing the Masses

People are drawn to stories. Narratives give context, offer a sense of purpose, and foster community. For opposition movements, a compelling story can inspire grassroots mobilization. It serves as the glue that binds disparate groups together, transforming them from isolated pockets of resistance into a formidable collective force. This unity can be instrumental in staging mass protests, boycotts, or other forms of civil disobedience.

3. Offering a Clear Vision

Merely highlighting the flaws of a strongman isn't a winning strategy. People yearn for hope and a promise of a better future. A counter-narrative needs to outline an alternative vision for the country – one that addresses the genuine grievances of the populace while promoting democratic values. By painting a picture of a prosperous, inclusive, and just nation, the opposition can present itself as a viable alternative, rather than just a dissenting voice.

4. Combatting Disinformation

One of the potent tools in a strongman's arsenal is disinformation. By muddying the waters and blurring the lines between fact and fiction, they can sow doubt and undermine trust in alternative sources of information. A unified counter-narrative, grounded in truth and transparency, can serve as an antidote. By consistently debunking falsehoods and promoting factual discourse, the opposition can cultivate trust among the populace.

5. Galvanizing International Support

In the global arena, narratives play a pivotal role in shaping perceptions. A strong, coherent counter-narrative can draw international attention to the strongman's transgressions. It can lead to international solidarity, with global actors – be it governments, NGOs, or the public – rallying behind the cause. This can translate into diplomatic pressure, economic sanctions, or support in terms of resources and expertise.

6. Preserving and Promoting Democratic Values

In the face of autocratic tendencies, it's crucial to remind the public of the core values at stake. Democracy, with its emphasis on freedom, equality, and justice, has an enduring appeal. A counter-narrative that champions these principles serves as a bulwark against the erosion of democratic norms. It instills a sense of pride in democratic traditions and emphasizes the importance of checks and balances, rule of law, and civil liberties.

7. Preparing for the Long Haul

Resistance against strongman regimes isn't a sprint; it's a marathon. Over the long haul, morale can waver, and fatigue can set in. A compelling counter-narrative serves as a constant source of inspiration. It reminds the opposition of the stakes, the ideals they're fighting for, and the vision they aim to realize. This sustenance is crucial to maintain momentum and ensure that the spirit of resistance remains undeterred.

Conclusion

In the battle against strongman rule, narratives are powerful weapons. While strongmen weave tales that consolidate their grip on power, the opposition's counter-narrative can be the catalyst for change. However, for this narrative to be effective, it must be more than just a rebuttal. It needs to be a clarion call that resonates with the masses, offering them a vision of hope, unity, and a brighter future. Only then can it truly challenge the allure of the strongman and pave the way for a democratic resurgence.

Chapter 10:
The Path Forward

Lessons from History: Preventing the Rise of Future Strongmen

Throughout history, nations have witnessed the ascent of strongmen who, riding waves of populism and discontent, have reshaped their political landscapes. These charismatic leaders often promise stability, prosperity, and a return to a glorified past, but at the cost of democratic values and institutions. As we look forward, it's vital to glean lessons from history to prevent a recurrence of such tendencies. Let's explore strategies to safeguard our democracies and preempt the rise of future strongmen.

1. Strengthening Democratic Institutions

A robust democracy rests on the pillars of its institutions, including the judiciary, media, and electoral bodies. These institutions act as checks and balances against unchecked power.

Lesson: Democracies should prioritize reinforcing these institutions, ensuring their independence and insulating them from political influence. A judiciary that can operate without interference, a media landscape that can report without intimidation, and electoral bodies that can function without bias are paramount.

2. Promoting Civic Education

One of the most potent defenses against autocratic tendencies is an informed and engaged citizenry.

Lesson: Introducing comprehensive civic education in schools can ensure that future generations understand their rights, the significance of democratic norms, and the dangers of unchecked power. Such education fosters critical thinking, enabling individuals to discern populist rhetoric from genuine leadership.

3. Ensuring Economic Stability

Economic distress often provides fertile ground for strongmen to emerge, capitalizing on grievances and promising rapid solutions.

Lesson: Governments should focus on inclusive economic policies that reduce inequalities, provide social safety nets, and promote sustainable growth. An economically content and hopeful populace is less likely to be swayed by the siren songs of demagogues.

4. Fostering National Unity

Strongmen often thrive in polarized environments, exploiting divisions and presenting themselves as the champions of particular groups.

Lesson: Promoting a narrative of national unity and shared destiny can counteract divisive rhetoric. Celebrating diversity while emphasizing common goals and values can help knit societies together.

5. Addressing Legitimate Concerns

Ignoring or trivializing genuine concerns, whether they relate to immigration, job loss, or cultural change, can lead to alienation. Strongmen can exploit this alienation.

Lesson: Governments must proactively address these concerns through dialogue, policies, and outreach. Engaging with citizens, understanding their fears, and devising holistic solutions can prevent feelings of disenfranchisement.

6. Regulating Information Flow

In the digital age, misinformation and propaganda spread rapidly, often fueling the rise of extremist views and leaders.

Lesson: While respecting freedom of expression, democracies should explore ways to combat the spread of deliberate falsehoods. This might include media literacy campaigns, fact-checking initiatives, and regulations on digital platforms to prevent the unchecked spread of misinformation.

7. Encouraging Political Pluralism

A vibrant democracy thrives on the presence of multiple voices and perspectives. Monolithic political landscapes, on the other hand, can pave the way for strongmen to consolidate power.

Lesson: Encouraging political pluralism, supporting diverse parties, and ensuring that electoral systems are fair and transparent can prevent the rise of authoritarian figures.

8. Global Cooperation

Strongmen often rise in tandem across regions, drawing inspiration and tactics from each other.

Lesson: Democracies around the world should collaborate, sharing best practices and strategies to safeguard their systems. International bodies can play a role in monitoring and intervening when democratic norms are threatened.

9. Remaining Vigilant

Complacency is democracy's enemy. Assuming that democratic systems are self-sustaining can lead to their erosion over time.

Lesson: Continuous vigilance, active civil society participation, and the willingness to reform and adapt are essential. Democracies should always be on the lookout for signs of erosion and be ready to act.

Conclusion

History, while replete with instances of strongmen altering the course of nations, also offers a wealth of lessons on resistance, resilience, and renewal. By heeding these lessons, democracies can fortify themselves, ensuring that they remain bastions of freedom, justice, and equality. The challenge lies not just in understanding history but in proactively shaping the future with its insights.

The Role of Education, Media Literacy, and Civic Engagement

As modern societies grapple with the challenges of political polarization, misinformation, and the potential rise of strongman leadership, the triad of education, media literacy, and civic engagement emerges as a vital force for strengthening democratic resilience. Each component serves as a building block for a well-informed and active citizenry, capable of discerning truth from falsehood and of ensuring that democratic principles are upheld. Let's delve deeper into the significance of each element in shaping the path forward.

1. Education: Laying the Foundation

At its core, education is about more than just imparting knowledge; it's about fostering critical thinking, promoting ethical values, and cultivating a sense of responsibility towards one's community and nation.

- **Empowerment Through Knowledge:** A solid educational foundation equips individuals with the tools to understand complex societal issues, from economics to political structures. It reduces vulnerabilities to populist rhetoric that often oversimplifies these complexities.

- **Ethical Grounding:** Educational institutions play a pivotal role in shaping an individual's moral compass. By instilling values of fairness, respect, and tolerance, education can act as a bulwark against divisive ideologies.

- **Encouraging Discourse:** Schools and colleges often serve as the first platforms for open discourse and debate. Encouraging these practices can cultivate a culture of dialogue over division, teaching young individuals to engage with opposing viewpoints constructively.

2. Media Literacy: Navigating the Information Deluge

In an era where information is abundant but often misleading, media literacy emerges as a crucial skill for the discerning citizen.

- **Distinguishing Fact from Fiction:** With the proliferation of digital platforms, distinguishing credible sources from unreliable ones becomes paramount. Media literacy equips individuals to identify biases, verify information, and understand the context.

- **Resisting Propaganda:** Strongman leaders often employ propaganda tools to bolster their narratives. A media-literate populace can recognize these tactics, reducing their efficacy.

- **Promoting Responsible Consumption:** Media literacy isn't just about critical consumption; it's also about responsible sharing. In the age of social media, unchecked sharing can amplify misinformation. Educating citizens about the implications of their digital actions is crucial.

3. Civic Engagement: Democracy in Action

Democracy thrives when its citizens are not just passive observers but active participants. Civic engagement encapsulates this participatory essence of democratic societies.

- **Understanding Rights and Responsibilities:** For a democracy to function optimally, its citizens need to be aware of their rights and responsibilities. This understanding ensures that individuals can both avail of the benefits of democracy and contribute to its functioning.

- **Engaging Beyond the Ballot Box:** While voting is a fundamental civic duty, engagement doesn't end there. Participating in community discussions, joining civil society organizations, or even engaging in peaceful protests are all facets of active civic participation.

- **Holding Power Accountable:** One of the core principles of democracy is the accountability of those in power. An engaged citizenry, well-versed in democratic norms, can serve as a potent check against potential abuses of power.

Integrating the Three for a Resilient Democracy

The confluence of education, media literacy, and civic engagement can fortify societies against the allure of strongman leaders and divisive ideologies. When citizens are educated, they can engage in informed debates; when they're media-literate, they can discern truth from propaganda; and when they're civically engaged, they can actively participate in shaping the course of their nation.

The Way Forward

Governments, educational institutions, civil society organizations, and even media entities have roles to play in promoting this triad:

- **Curriculum Reforms:** Incorporating media literacy into school curricula can ensure that future generations are equipped to navigate the digital information landscape.
- **Public Awareness Campaigns:** Governments and NGOs can run campaigns highlighting the importance of civic engagement, encouraging citizens to participate actively in democratic processes.
- **Platform Responsibility:** Digital platforms can contribute by flagging misinformation, promoting credible sources, and educating users about responsible content sharing.

Conclusion

The challenges posed by political polarization, misinformation, and the potential emergence of strongman leadership are significant. Yet, by investing in education, promoting media literacy, and encouraging civic engagement, societies can not only withstand these challenges but also emerge stronger. The path forward, while strewn with obstacles, is also illuminated by the promise of a more informed, engaged, and resilient citizenry.

Strengthening Institutions and Promoting Inclusive National Narratives

In the face of rising strongman tendencies, democracies are prompted to reflect on the health and resilience of their foundational institutions and the stories they tell about themselves. These institutions, from the judiciary to the press, serve as the bedrock upon which democratic societies are built. Similarly, the narratives nations embrace about their identity and values can either unite or divide. As such, fortifying these institutions and cultivating inclusive national narratives become paramount for a democracy's survival and prosperity.

1. Strengthening Democratic Institutions

The effectiveness and trustworthiness of democratic institutions directly impact the overall health of democracies. When these institutions are perceived as robust and impartial, the allure of authoritarian figures diminishes.

- **Fortifying the Rule of Law:** Trust in the judiciary is a cornerstone of any democracy. Courts must be seen as impartial arbiters, free from political influence. Enhancing judicial independence and ensuring timely and fair judicial processes can bolster public trust.

- **Independent Press:** A free and independent press serves as the fourth estate, holding power accountable and informing the public. Protecting journalists from intimidation, ensuring media ownership transparency, and promoting investigative journalism can reinforce the media's role in democracy.

- **Electoral Integrity:** Trust in the electoral process is foundational. Efforts must be made to ensure that elections are free, fair, and devoid of irregularities. This includes everything from securing voting systems against interference to ensuring that the public understands the electoral process.

- **Transparent Governance:** Trust is fostered when governments are transparent in their actions and decision-making processes. Implementing strong anti-corruption measures, promoting open government initiatives, and ensuring public officials are held accountable are vital steps.

2. Crafting Inclusive National Narratives

Beyond institutions, the narratives nations uphold about their identity, history, and values play a pivotal role in shaping public sentiment and cohesion.

- **Recognizing Diversity as Strength:** An inclusive national narrative acknowledges the diverse tapestry of backgrounds, cultures, and histories that make up a nation. Celebrating this diversity rather than viewing it as a threat can foster unity and mutual respect among citizens.

- **Revisiting Historical Narratives:** Often, national histories can be one-sided, neglecting the experiences of marginalized groups. An inclusive approach would involve revisiting these histories, incorporating diverse perspectives, and acknowledging past wrongs.

- **Promoting Shared Values:** While acknowledging diversity, it's crucial to also emphasize shared values and aspirations. This could include shared democratic principles, collective national achievements, or universal human rights ideals.

- **Encouraging Civic Participation:** A sense of ownership in the national narrative can be fostered by encouraging civic participation. This could involve community dialogues, citizen-led initiatives, or public consultations on matters of national importance.

3. The Role of Education in Shaping Narratives

Education systems play a significant role in shaping national narratives and promoting inclusive thinking.

- **Inclusive Curriculum:** School curricula can be designed to include diverse perspectives, histories, and cultures. This not only fosters respect among different groups but also provides a holistic view of national and world histories.

- **Promoting Critical Thinking:** Beyond content, the method of teaching is crucial. Encouraging critical thinking allows students to question, debate, and form their own informed opinions, rather than accepting information at face value.

- **Civic Education:** Educating students about democratic principles, rights, and responsibilities can instill a sense of civic duty and pride in democratic institutions.

4. The Media's Role in Shaping Narratives

The media holds immense power in crafting and disseminating national narratives.

- **Promoting Constructive Journalism:** Media outlets can prioritize stories that highlight unity, shared values, and positive community initiatives, thus promoting a sense of national cohesion.

- **Ensuring Diverse Representation:** Media representation matters. Ensuring that diverse voices, backgrounds, and perspectives are represented can lead to a more inclusive national dialogue.

Conclusion

As democracies navigate the challenges posed by rising strongman tendencies, the reinforcement of democratic institutions and the crafting of inclusive national narratives become imperative. While the journey is intricate, the destination is a resilient democracy characterized by strong institutions and a united, informed citizenry. The path forward calls for collective effort, introspection, and an unwavering commitment to the values that underpin democratic societies.

Conclusion

Reflecting on the Cyclical Nature of Strongmen in History

As we navigate through the annals of history, a recurring pattern emerges – the cyclical rise and fall of strongmen. These authoritative figures, with their magnetic charisma and promises of stability, have repeatedly emerged in times of societal unrest, only to fade away, often leaving nations in a more fractured state than before. Understanding this cyclical nature, recognizing the conditions that foster such rises, and reflecting on the aftermath is crucial in informing our contemporary responses and preparations for the future.

1. The Conditions for the Rise

Invariably, the ascent of strongmen has been predicated on a combination of economic downturns, perceived threats to cultural identity, and weakening trust in institutions.

- **Economic Turmoil:** Economic recessions, depressions, and widespread unemployment create a fertile ground for strongmen. The public, grappling with insecurity, is more receptive to leaders promising swift economic redress.

- **Identity and Cultural Threats:** Rapid demographic shifts, cultural changes, or perceived external threats can lead to a collective identity crisis. Strongmen often exploit such moments, projecting themselves as the defenders of traditional values and identity.

- **Distrust in Institutions:** When public trust in traditional institutions wanes – be it due to perceived ineffectiveness, corruption, or detachment from ordinary citizens – the allure of an authoritative figure who promises to "drain the swamp" or "clean the system" becomes irresistible to many.

2. The Strongman's Reign

Once in power, strongmen often employ similar tactics to consolidate their grip and neutralize opposition.

- **Centralization of Power:** One of the first moves often involves weakening checks and balances, centralizing authority, and eroding democratic institutions.
- **Control of Information:** The media and information outlets come under tight control, with dissenting voices silenced, marginalized, or discredited.
- **Creation of External Threats:** Strongmen frequently emphasize external threats – real or imagined – to rally domestic support and divert attention from internal issues.
- **Cult of Personality:** The leader is often elevated to an almost mythic status, with propaganda painting them as indispensable and irreplaceable.

3. The Aftermath

The reign of strongmen, no matter how long, often concludes with a set of common outcomes.

- **Economic and Social Turmoil:** The short-term stability or economic growth promised by strongmen frequently gives way to long-term economic mismanagement and social unrest.
- **Institutional Erosion:** The weakened democratic institutions, after years of erosion, often struggle to regain public trust and effectiveness.
- **Polarized Society:** The divisive tactics and "us vs. them" rhetoric leave societies deeply polarized, requiring significant efforts to heal and rebuild.

4. Reflections for the Present

While history offers numerous examples of the rise and fall of strongmen, the contemporary world presents its own unique challenges and variables.

- **The Role of Technology:** Modern technology, especially social media, amplifies the reach and influence of potential strongmen. The rapid spread of misinformation and the creation of echo chambers further bolster their appeal.

- **Globalization:** In our interconnected world, the actions of strongmen have ripple effects far beyond their borders. Whether it's economic policies or diplomatic relations, the global community is more intertwined than ever.
- **Resilient Democracies:** On a positive note, many modern democracies have developed mechanisms and safeguards based on past experiences. These institutional safeguards, combined with a vigilant civil society, can act as bulwarks against the unchecked rise of authoritarian figures.

5. Preparing for the Future

Recognizing the cyclical nature of strongmen is the first step towards preparing for, and potentially averting, future occurrences.

- **Strengthening Institutions:** The emphasis should be on bolstering democratic institutions, ensuring their transparency, effectiveness, and independence.
- **Promoting Civic Education:** An informed and engaged citizenry is one of the best defenses against the rise of strongmen. A focus on civic education, critical thinking, and media literacy can play a pivotal role.
- **Fostering Inclusion:** Adopting inclusive national narratives, acknowledging and celebrating diversity, and ensuring that all sections of society feel represented and heard can diminish the appeal of divisive figures.

Conclusion

History, with its cyclical patterns, serves as both a cautionary tale and a guide. The rise and fall of strongmen, a recurring theme, prompts introspection and proactive measures. By understanding the conditions that give rise to such figures, recognizing their tactics, and reflecting on the aftermath, societies can better equip themselves to navigate these challenges and foster a more inclusive, resilient, and democratic future. The lessons from the past, combined with the tools and knowledge of the present, provide hope for a world where the allure of strongmen diminishes in the face of robust democracies and an empowered citizenry.

The Ongoing Struggle Between Complexity and Simplicity in Democratic Societies

Democracy, in its essence, is a complex and delicate balancing act. It thrives on checks and balances, diverse viewpoints, multifaceted institutions, and the active participation of its citizenry. Yet, the very intricacies that make democracies robust also make them vulnerable to the allure of simplicity, particularly in moments of societal upheaval. The interplay between complexity and simplicity has always been at the heart of democratic systems, and understanding this tension is vital for the resilience and evolution of democracies.

1. The Nature of Complexity in Democracies

Democracies, by design, embrace complexity:

- **Pluralism:** They celebrate the coexistence of multiple identities, beliefs, and perspectives. This plurality enriches public discourse but also makes consensus-building challenging.

- **Institutional Framework:** Democracies operate through a web of institutions, each with its role and jurisdiction, ensuring power isn't concentrated and that rights are protected. But this decentralization can sometimes lead to inefficiencies and bureaucratic delays.

- **Rule of Law:** Democratic societies prioritize the rule of law, which can be intricate, ensuring fairness and justice. However, legal complexities can sometimes feel overwhelming to ordinary citizens.

2. The Allure of Simplicity

Against this backdrop, the appeal of simplicity emerges powerfully:

- **Clear Answers:** In a world of nuance, ambiguity, and protracted debates, straightforward answers—even if reductive—resonate. Simple solutions are often more digestible, even if they bypass the intricacies of the problem.

- **Unified Narratives:** A single, cohesive narrative can be more appealing than a cacophony of diverse voices, especially during crises when people seek clarity and direction.

- **Decisive Action:** In the face of perceived threats or challenges, swift and decisive actions, even if they sideline democratic norms, can attract support from those feeling anxious or impatient.

3. The Strongman as the Embodiment of Simplicity

Often, strongmen or authoritarian-leaning leaders present themselves as the antidotes to democratic complexities:

- **Monolithic Narratives:** They frequently offer singular visions of national identity, sidelining pluralism.

- **Centralization of Power:** Promising efficiency, they might bypass institutional checks, centralizing authority and decision-making.

- **Populist Appeals:** Playing on widespread sentiments, they often use populist rhetoric that promises to cut through bureaucratic red tape and directly address the people's needs.

4. The Dangers of Oversimplification

While simplicity has its allure, its unchecked embrace can imperil democracies:

- **Loss of Nuance:** Simplistic solutions might not address the root causes of problems, leading to unintended consequences or exacerbating issues.

- **Erosion of Rights:** The sidelining of complexity can mean the sidelining of minority rights, undermining the very essence of democratic inclusivity.

- **Institutional Decay:** Bypassing democratic institutions for the sake of efficiency or simplicity can weaken them in the long run, making democracies vulnerable to authoritarian tendencies.

5. Embracing Complexity: A Democratic Imperative

For democracies to thrive, there's a need to recognize and appreciate their inherent complexities:

- **Educating the Citizenry:** A well-informed public that understands the intricacies of democratic governance is less likely to fall for reductive solutions. Civic education, media literacy, and critical thinking become essential.

- **Inclusive Deliberation:** Encouraging broad-based public deliberations ensures that multiple voices are heard, and complexities are acknowledged.

- **Transparent Institutions:** Making institutions transparent and accountable can mitigate feelings of alienation and reduce the appeal of oversimplified solutions.

6. Navigating the Balance

Striking the right balance between complexity and simplicity is a dynamic process:

- **Adaptive Governance:** Democracies must be nimble, adapting to changing circumstances without compromising on core principles.

- **Responsive Institutions:** While maintaining their integrity, democratic institutions should be responsive, addressing people's concerns efficiently.

- **Engaged Leadership:** Leaders play a pivotal role in bridging the gap between complexity and simplicity, translating intricate issues into relatable narratives without resorting to reductionism.

Conclusion

The tension between complexity and simplicity isn't new, but in an age of rapid information dissemination and global interconnectivity, its implications are profound. Democracies, with their multifaceted nature, face the challenge of ensuring that their complexities are not their undoing. By acknowledging this tension, continuously educating the citizenry, ensuring transparent governance, and fostering inclusive narratives, democracies can navigate the delicate balance, ensuring that the allure of simplicity doesn't overshadow the richness of democratic complexity. The ongoing struggle is emblematic of the broader challenges democracies face, and how they address it will shape their resilience and vibrancy in the years to come.

A Call to Action: Engage, Educate, and Actively Participate in Your Democracy

As we reflect on the complexities and challenges posed by strongmen and the appeal of oversimplified solutions, it becomes clear that democracy is not a passive system. It requires the active engagement of its citizenry. The health, resilience, and vitality of democratic societies depend on the informed and active participation of its members. It's not just about voting once every few years; it's about becoming a continuous participant in the democratic process.

1. The Power of Individual Engagement

Democracy is not a spectator sport. It thrives when individuals recognize their agency and actively involve themselves in the decision-making processes:

- **Informed Voting:** Beyond just casting a ballot, it's vital to be informed about candidates, their policies, and the broader implications of electoral choices.
- **Community Involvement:** Democracy happens at all levels. Getting involved in local governance, community boards, or

neighborhood councils can make tangible differences in daily lives.

- **Public Discourse:** Engaging in public discussions, attending town halls, or even organizing public forums can provide platforms to discuss, debate, and dissect issues affecting the community.

2. The Imperative of Education

Education is the cornerstone of a resilient democracy:

- **Civic Education:** Understanding the workings of democratic institutions, the principles of the rule of law, and the importance of checks and balances arms citizens against potential authoritarian tendencies.

- **Media Literacy:** In an era of information overload, discerning fact from fiction is crucial. Educating oneself about reliable news sources, fact-checking, and critical thinking can guard against misinformation and propaganda.

- **History Lessons:** Understanding historical precedents, both of democratic triumphs and authoritarian regimes, provides context for current events and a roadmap for future challenges.

3. Participation Beyond the Ballot Box

Active participation extends beyond just electoral processes:

- **Volunteering:** Working with NGOs, community organizations, or advocacy groups amplifies voices and drives change at grassroots levels.

- **Supporting Independent Media:** A free press is a pillar of democracy. Supporting independent journalism ensures a flow of unbiased information, holding power to account.

- **Petitions and Protests:** Leveraging tools of direct democracy, like petitions or peaceful protests, can highlight issues and put pressure on elected officials.

4. The Digital Frontier

The digital age offers both challenges and opportunities for democratic engagement:

- **Digital Platforms:** Use social media responsibly. Share verified information, engage in constructive debates, and use online platforms to mobilize support for democratic causes.
- **Stay Alert to Manipulation:** Be aware of the pitfalls of echo chambers, misinformation campaigns, and foreign interference. Digital literacy is as vital as traditional media literacy.
- **Connect Globally:** The internet bridges geographical divides. Engage with global communities, share experiences, and learn from democracies around the world.

5. The Importance of Solidarity

Democracies thrive on collective strength:

- **Allyship:** Stand in solidarity with marginalized groups. The erosion of one group's rights can be a precursor to broader democratic decay.
- **Intercommunity Dialogues:** Foster conversations between different community groups. Breaking down silos and dispelling myths strengthens the social fabric.
- **International Solidarity:** Democracies aren't isolated entities. Support democratic movements worldwide, recognizing that global democratic health impacts all democracies.

6. Continuous Vigilance

The price of liberty is eternal vigilance:

- **Hold Leaders Accountable:** Elected officials are public servants. Continuously scrutinize their actions, ask tough questions, and demand transparency and accountability.
- **Guard Against Complacency:** Democracy can be eroded subtly. Stay alert to signs of decay, and be ready to mobilize against any threats to democratic norms.

- **Celebrate Democracy:** While it's essential to be vigilant, also celebrate democratic milestones, successes, and everyday democratic processes. Joy and celebration can be as potent as protest.

Conclusion

At its heart, democracy is a collective endeavor, an ongoing project shaped by its participants. It's not static; it evolves, adapts, and grows with the active involvement of its citizens. As we've seen through history, democracies can be both robust and fragile. Their resilience depends on the informed and active participation of people like you.

So, as we conclude our exploration, the call to action is clear: Engage. Educate. Act. Your voice, your involvement, and your commitment are the lifeblood of democracy. Embrace that power, wield it responsibly, and be the change you wish to see in your democratic society. The future of democracy is in your hands.

Appendix A: Profiles of modern-day strongmen in the West

The rise of strongmen in the West, figures who prioritize personal power and direct leadership over democratic processes and norms, has been a notable trend in recent years. These leaders, often charismatic and controversial, appeal to a significant portion of the electorate by promising simple solutions to complex problems and championing a return to "better days." This appendix provides an overview of a few such figures, examining their backgrounds, their tactics, and their impact on the Western political landscape.

1. Donald Trump (United States)

Background: Donald J. Trump, before his political career, was best known as a real estate mogul and reality TV star. In 2016, he secured the U.S. presidency as a Republican, defeating Democratic candidate Hillary Clinton.

Tactics and Leadership Style

Populist Rhetoric: Trump's "Make America Great Again" slogan encapsulated his appeal to those who felt left behind in modern America.

Media Mastery: Trump is notorious for his use of Twitter, bypassing traditional media to speak directly to his supporters.

Polarization: Trump often engaged in us-versus-them rhetoric, particularly targeting immigrants, the media, and the "deep state."

Impact: Trump's presidency was marked by significant policy shifts, especially in areas like immigration, environmental regulations, and foreign policy. His tenure deepened the political divide in the U.S., with many praising his "straight-talk" and others decrying his challenges to democratic norms.

2. Viktor Orbán (Hungary)

Background: Orbán has been a dominant figure in Hungarian politics for decades, first serving as Prime Minister from 1998 to 2002 and then returning to the post in 2010, where he remains as of this writing.

Tactics and Leadership Style

Nationalist Appeal: Orbán frequently emphasizes Hungary's Christian identity and its need for protection against external threats, particularly from Muslim migrants.

Control Over Media: Under Orbán, many media outlets in Hungary have come under the control of his allies, limiting critical voices.

Constitutional Changes: Orbán's party, Fidesz, has implemented significant changes to the Hungarian constitution, concentrating power and weakening checks and balances.

Impact: Hungary, under Orbán, has faced criticism from other European Union nations for perceived authoritarian tendencies and challenges to the rule of law.

3. Jair Bolsonaro (Brazil)

Background: A former military officer, Bolsonaro became Brazil's president in 2019, positioning himself as a political outsider ready to challenge the status quo.

Tactics and Leadership Style:

Tough on Crime: Bolsonaro's commitment to addressing Brazil's high crime rates with strong police actions attracted many voters.

Anti-Corruption Stance: Running on an anti-corruption platform, he promised to clean up politics in Brazil, a country that had been rocked by corruption scandals.

Controversial Remarks: Bolsonaro is known for his provocative statements, often on topics like gender, indigenous rights, and the environment.

Impact: Bolsonaro's leadership has been polarizing, with some praising his strongman tactics and others alarmed by his dismissal of environmental concerns and his handling of the COVID-19 pandemic.

4. Recep Tayyip Erdoğan (Turkey)

Background: Erdoğan has been a leading figure in Turkish politics since the early 2000s, first as Prime Minister and later as President.

Tactics and Leadership Style:

Religious Conservatism: Erdoğan's leadership has marked a shift toward more conservative Islamic values in Turkey.

Suppressing Dissent: Numerous journalists, academics, and political opponents have been arrested during Erdoğan's tenure.

Constitutional Power Grabs: Erdoğan has overseen significant changes to Turkey's constitution, notably a 2017 referendum that expanded presidential powers.

Impact: Under Erdoğan, Turkey has drifted away from its secularist roots, and its relationships with Western powers have become more strained, particularly given concerns over human rights and democratic backsliding.

Conclusion

The rise of these modern-day strongmen underscores a broader global trend: the appeal of authoritative leaders who promise stability, strength, and a return to perceived "golden eras." Their leadership styles, often marked by populism, nationalism, and a challenge to established democratic norms, present both challenges and opportunities for the future of Western democracies.

Appendix B: Further reading and resources

The rise and dynamics of strongmen in Western democracies is a complex topic that demands a deep and varied exploration. For those interested in diving deeper, this appendix provides a curated list of books, articles, documentaries, and online resources that offer a comprehensive understanding of the phenomenon.

1. Books

"How Democracies Die" by Steven Levitsky and Daniel Ziblatt

A deep dive into the subtle and not-so-subtle ways in which democratic institutions can be undermined from within. The authors provide a comparative analysis of democratic backsliding, drawing lessons from various countries.

"The Road to Unfreedom: Russia, Europe, America" by Timothy Snyder

This book traces the global rise of authoritarianism and offers an exploration into the tactics used by authoritarian leaders, from propaganda to violence.

"The People vs. Democracy: Why Our Freedom Is in Danger and How to Save It" by Yascha Mounk

Mounk discusses the growing disillusionment with liberal democracies and the allure of populist leaders, presenting both a diagnosis and potential solutions.

"What Is Populism?" by Jan-Werner Müller

A concise exploration into the phenomenon of populism, this book differentiates between left-wing and right-wing populisms and examines their implications for modern democracies.

2. Articles

"The Strongman Problem, from Modi to Trump" in **The New Yorker**

This piece offers a global perspective on the rise of strongman leaders, drawing parallels and contrasts among various countries.

"The Autocrat's Playbook" in **The Atlantic**

An examination of the tactics used by autocratic leaders to consolidate power and suppress opposition.

"Populism Isn't Going Away" in **Foreign Affairs**

A comprehensive analysis of the lasting allure of populist politics and its implications for global democracy.

3. Documentaries

"The Edge of Democracy"

This Netflix documentary offers an intimate look at Brazil's political upheavals, tracing the rise of Jair Bolsonaro against the backdrop of political corruption and social unrest.

"Putin's Revenge"

Produced by PBS's FRONTLINE, this two-part series delves into Vladimir Putin's journey from the KGB to the Russian presidency, providing insight into his motivations and tactics.

"Trump's Takeover"

Another FRONTLINE production, this documentary offers a behind-the-scenes look at Donald Trump's first year in the White House, focusing on his style of governance and his relationship with the Republican Party.

4. Online Resources

Freedom House Reports

https://freedomhouse.org produces annual reports on the state of global freedom, including analyses of democratic backsliding and the rise of authoritarianism.

Varieties of Democracy (V-Dem)

The https://www.v-dem.net/en provides a comprehensive dataset on democracy, offering tools to track the ebb and flow of democratic norms across countries and over time.

The Global Populism Database

An initiative by researchers at the University of Georgia and the University of Oslo, this database (https://thegpdatabase.com/) offers metrics on populist discourse in the political speeches of executive chief executives from around the world.

5. Academic Journals

"Journal of Democracy"

A quarterly publication, the Journal of Democracy offers articles and essays on the theory and practice of democracy, including challenges and potential reforms.

"Democratization"

This journal focuses on the complexities of transitions from authoritarian rule to democratic governance, providing case studies and theoretical insights.

Conclusion

The resources provided here offer just a glimpse into the vast amount of material available on the topic of strongmen and the challenges facing Western democracies. Continuous education and engagement are key to understanding and ultimately addressing the rise of these leaders. As democratic citizens, equipping ourselves with knowledge is the first step in ensuring the health and longevity of our institutions.